WHAT OTHERS ARE SAYING

Seeking a deeper relationship with God takes you to a new level of his glory. Sherry Conrad has experienced the manifestation of God's glory here on earth and releases heavenly revelation throughout her book. After reading this book you will have tools that will give you insight to the supernatural realm and find yourself daily having encounters with God. I am a testimony on how God uses Sherry Conrad to pull songs of revelation from Heaven to bring healing to my life!

—Pastor Victoria Swisher
FUEL Youth Ministry
Hayesville, North Carolina

Be prepared to have your spiritual eyes opened to the reality of God speaking to you through prophetic dreams and visions. Sherry Conrad, a life-long student of the Bible and woman of tried faith, makes decoding those vague recollections after the morning alarm simple, with often astounding results. Guidance, wisdom, understanding, and long sought-after answers are being revealed to you in your sleep. Learning to interpret what the Spirit of the Lord is saying will deepen your faith and give you a better understanding of how closely the Lord walks with you daily. Mrs. Conrad, who shares the wonderful testimony of the love and ever-present hand of God on her life, will show you quick, simple, accurate ways to see into the symbolic representations in your dreams.

—Associate Pastors Shep and Stacy Calhoun
Living Word Revival Center
Hayesville, North Carolina

We are living in "the Best of times and the Worst of times" and God has given us insights and revelations for the comfort and assurance we so desperately need. In her book "God's Insight for Your Life through Dreams & Visions, Sherry Conrad has presented valuable information and revelation for our navigation through life's challenges in the Last Day. Daniel (12:4, 8-9) and (Amos 3:7) both present the message that in these Last Days Prophetic voices will bring forth revelation, inspiration and understandings of God's Plan and Strategies for the equipping of believers for victory. Sherry Conrad is one of these fresh Prophetic voices. I therefore highly recommend this book for your study, enlightenment, and enjoyment.

—Pastors Ed and Judy DeWitt
Living Word Revival Center
Hayesville, North Carolina

The word of God says in Hosea that his people perish for lack of knowledge, this book could become a good source of information to help someone understand symbolisms used in the Bible, prophecy, dreams & visions. As a teacher and intercessor it is a very valuable tool to have to interpret what we hear the Lord say or what we dream about or to understand the visions we get. When we understand the symbolisms it is easier and more effective when we are praying or teaching about the subject of the prophecy's, dreams or visions we receive. This is a great tool to help the body of Christ to gain more knowledge and understanding of God and his ways.

In Christ,
Pastor Gary Howard & Prophet Elizabeth Howard
Living Word Revival Center
Hayesville, North Carolina

It is true, God speaks through visions and dreams, but He's not just expressing Himself for nothing. I often tell people everywhere that one thing you can't take away from a person is their experience, especially if they've experienced God. God's Insight for Your Life Through Dreams and Visions, will trigger the necessary foundation to provide you with the Insight you need to gain practical foresight, direction and courage to become aware of Why He speaks through dreams. In my bedroom I have one bookshelf of what I call "necessary hands-on-material" which provides me with reference material to support my erratic moments of insight. This is the kind of book that would be on that shelf. I not only suggest this book for reading, but as a reference guide and handbook. Sherry Conrad has tapped into the realms of worship and prophetic insight that will build your life and awareness. Get ready to be impacted!

B.Dwayne Hardin, Apostle & Pastor
The Embassy
Atlanta, GA

God's
INSIGHT FOR
YOUR LIFE THROUGH
DREAMS AND VISIONS

SHERRY CONRAD

God's INSIGHT FOR YOUR LIFE THROUGH DREAMS AND VISIONS

God Bless You!

Sherry Conrad

Acts 2:17

TATE PUBLISHING
AND ENTERPRISES, LLC

Published by Tate Publishing & Enterprises, LLC
127 E. Trade Center Terrace | Mustang, Oklahoma 73064 USA
1.888.361.9473 | www.tatepublishing.com

Tate Publishing is committed to excellence in the publishing industry. The company reflects the philosophy established by the founders, based on Psalm 68:11,
"The Lord gave the word and great was the company of those who published it."

Book design copyright © 2013 by Tate Publishing, LLC. All rights reserved.
Cover design by Arjay Grecia
Interior design by Jomar Ouano

Published in the United States of America

ISBN: 978-1-62854-890-7
1. Religion / Christian Life / General
2. Religion / Christian Life / Personal Growth
13.11.01

DEDICATION

This book is dedicated to my Lord and Savior Jesus Christ, who is the love of my life. He is the very reason I breathe, he is the song I sing, all that I have been blessed with is from you alone Jesus. I place my life within your hands, knowing that you are molding me into your image and you are taking me to places that I have never been before. As I look back upon my life I see where you have taken me from glory to glory. I place you first in my life forevermore. If you have never met Jesus take this moment right now, for we are not promised tomorrow and this life is but a vapor, time passes by so fast you just never know when your time is up. I decree that you will acknowledge your imperfections and receive Jesus Christ as Lord of your life, as you cast all of your cares at the feet of Jesus know that all of your sins are washed away by his blood. Pray this *prayer* meaning every word from your spirit, inviting Jesus into your life as your Lord and Savior understanding that God loves you so very much and that his Son Jesus sacrificed his life for you. Know that Jesus is the Son of God, and that when you believe in Jesus as Lord of your life placing him first and foremost above everything else in your life, you will have everlasting life. Show your obedience to the Lord by being baptized by water. Jesus was baptized and many other people have been as well, since Jesus has shown us this example to follow we should be obedient and follow his ways. All of Heaven is rejoicing once you become an ambassador of the kingdom of God.

"Father, I know that I have broken your laws and my sins have separated me from you. I am truly sorry, and now I want to turn away from my past sinful life toward you. Please forgive me, and help me avoid sinning again. I believe that your son, Jesus Christ died for my sins, was resurrected from the dead, is alive, and hears my prayer. I invite Jesus to become the Lord of my life to rule and reign in my heart from this day forward. Please send your Holy Spirit to help me obey you, and to do your will for the rest of my life. In Jesus' name I pray. Amen."

That's *fantastic, welcome to the kingdom of God!* Now find a church that teaches the word of God from the Holy Bible. I personally suggest the King James Version, for you to study. Once you find a church home, serving in the house of the Lord is a terrific way to show not only Jesus how much you love him, but it is another way to show Jesus how much you love yourself and other people as well. Share your excitement about your decision of becoming an ambassador of the kingdom of God with your Pastor and ask your Pastor about scheduling a water baptism. Baptism in the holy bible was by immersion, that is, the person went fully under the waters. Jesus told us that we must be *born again* to enter into Heaven for eternity: *"Verily, verily, I say unto thee, Except a man be born of water and of the Spirit, he cannot enter into the kingdom of God. That which is born of the flesh is flesh; and that which is born of the Spirit is spirit. Marvel not that I said unto thee, Ye must be born again. The wind bloweth where it listeth, and thou hearest the sound thereof, but canst not tell whence it cometh, and whither it goeth: so is every one that is born of the Spirit."*[1] Jesus demonstrated by his baptism, that he was committed to doing his Father's will, he is our perfect model. As we see in (Mathew 3:13-17), Then cometh Jesus from Galilee to Jordan unto John, to be baptized of him. But John forbad him, saying, *"I have need to be baptized of thee, and comest thou to me?"* And Jesus answering said unto him, *"Suffer it to be so now; for thus it becometh us to fulfil all righteousness."* Then he suffered him. And Jesus, when he was baptized, went straightway out of the water: and lo, the heavens were opened unto him, and he saw the Spirit of God descending like a dove, and lightning upon him: And lo a voice from heaven, saying, *"This is my beloved Son, in whom I am well pleased."*

I am not saying that water baptism is required for salvation, I know that there are people who believe that you must be baptized to go to Heaven please refer to the thief who expressed his faith to Jesus while hanging beside him on the cross. And he said unto Jesus, *"Lord, remember me when thou comest into thy kingdom."* And Jesus said unto him, *"Verily I say unto thee, Today shall thou be with me in paradise."*[2] This thief was never baptized, and yet Jesus assured him that he would join him in paradise. Faith that Jesus is Lord is God's faithful promise to you that will assure your eternity in Heaven. Your works speak to the degree of your faith in Jesus Christ and your obedience to walk out the call that God has placed upon your life. One important fact about the thief is his lack of baptism was not a result of disobedience. The thief found salvation at that moment, while hanging beside Jesus on the cross, the thief never had the opportunity for baptism. Just stop disagreeing with Jesus, and get baptized. Jesus said it so do it!

Jesus told us: *"Not everyone that saith unto me, Lord, Lord, shall enter into kingdom of heaven; but he that doeth the will of my Father which is in heaven. Many will say to me in that day, Lord, Lord, have we not prophesied in thy name? And in thy name have cast out devils? And in thy name done many wonderful works? And then will I profess unto them, I never knew you: depart from me, ye that work iniquity."*[3] The will of the Father in Heaven is for you to repent of your sins and walk in righteousness with him. Having a relationship with God is the key to finding your way to Heaven, Jesus said, *"Enter ye at the strait gate: for wide is the gate, and broad is the way, that leadeth to destruction, and many there be which go in thereat: Because strait is the gate: and narrow is the way, which leadeth unto life, and few there be that find it.*[4] Read the holy bible every day; come before God giving him all praise, honor, and glory worshipping the Lord in spirit and in truth. God loves to hear you thank him for the blessings that he has placed upon your life, remember the Apostle James tells us: *"Every good gift and every perfect gift is from above, and cometh down from the Father of lights, with whom is no variableness, neither shadow of turning."*[5] Build a relationship with Jesus he is waiting for you with his arms open wide ready to embrace you, enter into his love where you belong, with his arms of love wrapped around you for all of eternity. God bless you!

I would also like to dedicate this book to my husband Steven and my five children, Nicole, Melissa, Andrew, Christina and Isaac. I decree this to God over all of your lives, you are a new creation in Christ; old things have passed away and all things have become new.[6] You are the salt of the earth.[7] You are united to the Lord and are one spirit with Him.[8] You are a chosen generation, a royal priesthood, a holy nation.[9] You are part of the bride of Christ and are making yourself ready for Him.[10] I love you all and thank you for your understanding as I have diligently pressed forward into this journey that God has taken me through. We have all grown much closer to God and I thank God, for you all are truly blessings from God.

I dedicate this book to my parents, Edward and Peggy Laney. They are truly a blessing from God in my life. My parents have a reverence for God always placing God first in their lives and they have taught their children to reverence God as well. When I think about my parents I think about the love of God that they have given to me, by placing the word of God within my hands when I was only 6 years old, I received my first bible from my parents on August 28, 1972, a child is never too young to start reading the word of God. Growing up in Christ Jesus, consisted of Sunday school every Sunday, I always looked forward to learning more about God, and all of the amazing stories that are in the bible. God used so many different people in many ways to share his love. I honor and respect my parents and continually keep them in my prayers as I pray to God. I thank God everyday for my parents who are not ashamed of God and are always ready to share his love with others, when you look at them the love of God shines from them. They are an example to me of God's love. God bless you always, Dad and Mom, I love you.

ACKNOWLEDGMENTS

Forever and ever and ever: Written by Sherry A. Conrad on 9/18/10, Melody by Sherry A. Conrad, Lead Vocals: Adam Benedict & Sherry A. Conrad, Keyboard: Adam Benedict

The Gates of Heaven: Written by Sherry A. Conrad on 3/10/08, Melody by Sherry A. Conrad, Lead Vocal: Sherry A. Conrad, Keyboard: Adam Benedict, Background Vocals: Adam Benedict, Andrew Conrad, Christina Conrad, Tina Lundy and Vernois Wilson.

Tears from Heaven: Written by Sherry A. Conrad on 9/16/10, Melody by Sherry A. Conrad, Lead Vocals: Sherry A. Conrad & Josh Del Cid, Keyboard: Josh Del Cid.

The Spirit of the Lord is in the Bride: Written by Sherry A. Conrad on 6/22/09, this song is sung acapello, Lead Vocal: Sherry A. Conrad.

Angels: Written by Sherry A. Conrad on 4/8/11, Melody by Sherry A. Conrad, Lead Vocals: Sherry A. Conrad, Keyboard: Sherry A. Conrad, Background Vocals: Adam Benedict and Vernois Wilson.

I would like to give special recognition to Pastor Victoria Swisher of FUEL Youth Ministry in Hayesville, NC. She helped me with the recording of these songs; thank you and God bless you abundantly!

I would like to give special recognition to Apostle's Steven and Valerie Swisher of Living Word Revival Center in Hayesville, NC. They allowed me to use their church and the equipment at the church to record my music for this book, God bless you abundantly, thanks!

I would like thank all of the musicians that worked diligently taking their time to help play music and sing all of these songs that the Lord has released to me:

Adam Benedict: He is a Praise and Worship Leader at Living Word Revival Center, Hayesville, NC. Keyboard, Drums, Guitar and Lead Vocal, thank you for using your talent and time for this project, God will bless you abundantly!

Josh Del Cid: Thank you for using your talent and time for this project, God will bless you abundantly! Check out Josh's music page @ visit: http://www.facebook.com/josuedelcidmusic.

Josh travels to the Nations ministering the word of God!

Tina Lundy: Thank you for using your talent and time for this project, God will bless you abundantly!

Vernois Wilson: She is a Praise and Worship Leader at Living Word Revival Center, Hayesville, NC. Lead Vocal and background vocals. Thank you for using your talent and time for this project, God will bless you abundantly!

Special thanks to my children who have taken their time to sing: Andrew Conrad and Christina Conrad, you are both blessings from God. I decree that the Lord's hand is upon your life and that he is guiding you all the days of your life. Let this experience never depart from your lives, always growing closer to God, I love you both, God bless you always, love Mom.

CONTENTS

FOREWORD

There is a fresh release of the Kingdom in these days, it's filled with dreams and visions so that we may experience Heaven on Earth. In our everyday lives we are given ample opportunities to walk out our destiny. We look at ourselves as just everyday soccer moms in route to a game, an office administrator who is feeling like everyday at the office is just another day at the office or that missionary who is called to the nations of the world and is still waiting for the ticket. No matter what it is you are fulfilling that day, God wants us to do it in the fullness of the understanding of what it is he is speaking to us in his dreams, visions and symbols in our lives today.

Sherry Conrad is anointed for this time to release a prophetic understanding of dreams and visions through the word and spirit that is being released to God's people in this hour. I have known Sherry for over seven years, and in those seven years it has been a privilege to stand by her side and benefited greatly from the prophetic insight she has received from God. Sherry and her husband Steven have been married 24 years and they have five children, two in college, and two in elementary school and one still at home. I have watched Sherry impart and release the understanding of the kingdom into her children. In doing so it has opened their eyes and ears to the heavenly understanding through dreams and visions. In this year her son Andrew who is 10 has asked God to show him Heaven, and her son Andrew was taken to Heaven and when he shared his experience there was no fear but complete understanding of the fullness of what God was showing him. I encourage you to prepare yourself to be forever changed and to daily apply the understanding you will receive as you read this book.

So sit down, put on your seat belt because you are about to take a journey you have only dreamt about. After reading this book, you will not only have dreams but *understand* what God is showing you! *"And it shall be in the last days God says that I will pour out my Spirit on all mankind (Acts 2:17)."*

From the fire in the mountains,
Apostle's Steven and Valerie Swisher
Living Word Revival Center/M.A.P. International
Hayesville, NC.

PREFACE

I began to write this book after the reality of meeting Jesus face to
face saturated my entire being, I couldn't deny this encounter with
Jesus any longer. Through this experience I began to understand
who I was created to be through him. I had not only seen him
with my own two eyes, I experienced the sound of his voice
illuminating my mind, and I stood in the manifest presence of his
glory, being forever changed by his love for me. No matter how
hard I tried to suppress this encounter with Jesus I just couldn't
forget him. He had opened my mind to a deeper revelation of
who he is to me, renewing a passion in my spirit that longed to
be with him, to never ever leave him. You are probably asking
yourself why would she want to forget about meeting Jesus? The
reason that I tried to forget was because I had forgotten who I
was, hence forgetting who Jesus is, he is the Christ the Savior of
the world. I had forgotten Jesus however, Jesus never forgot me.
I asked Jesus, "With all of the people in this world why would
you take time for me Jesus?" I will share with you why Jesus chose
me to share this with you, as you begin to walk with me through
this journey with Jesus, ask yourself why not me Jesus? Jesus
imparted so much wisdom to me that day and I began to see and
understand this wisdom in many different aspects of my life. Let
me make one important fact clear to you, I am of a sound mind,
I know what I see and hear, I am very aware of my surroundings.
Let me give you an analogy of how we see things in this world,

when I was fifteen years old, I was old enough to take a test to get my restricted driver's license so that I could drive with an adult. I took the written test and passed it, and then I had one more test to take the vision test. As I looked into the binoculars to read the words I couldn't see the words that were far away. I failed the vision part of my test and was told that I needed to have my eyes examined and that I could come back once I had my vision corrected and retake the vision test. I stopped in shock at this news, my entire life up until this point I thought I was seeing just fine, turns out not everyone sees everything the same way. I went to the eye doctor he examined my eyes; I purchased contacts and left the doctor's office. I couldn't believe what I was seeing, the world was so new to me, I was able to see things that I had never seen before even though I had been there before. I thought I was seeing to my full potential that was until I placed those corrective lenses in my eyes. Let me ask you this do you see everything in your life to your full potential? Allow the love of Jesus to open your eyes to a deeper revelation of who he is, of how he wants you to see him. Step into my life and I will take you on my journey with Jesus as I begin to understand just how much Jesus loves me. Why would you want to step into my life and embark on this journey? You will have a greater understanding of who you are once you understand how much Jesus loves you. Once you understand there is only one you. Once you understand you were made for such a time as this. Are you longing to understand a dream you had last year and you keep longing to understand that one part of that dream and you just can't grasp the meaning of this dream? I have spent years studying the word of God and how God uses symbols to get an idea across to us. In this book you will be able to break down dreams and visions that God has released to me, filling in the blanks with discernment from the word of God. As you go through these exercises of how to interpret a dream or vision use the symbolic dictionary that is included with this book to help you discern these dreams and visions. God has released many dreams to me over my lifetime and this is how God speaks with me. A lot of our understanding of dreams and visions are relevant to who God has called us to be in our lifetime. I will teach you how God speaks with me and how you will be able to use this teaching in your life to awaken the call that God has for your life.

I would recommend this teaching to everyone; your parents for God says that he will pour out his spirit in the latter days and that your old men will dream dreams and your children will see visions. We are in the latter days, that God speaks of in his word; it is imperative that we begin to understand why and how God speaks with us. Our parents are not only the generation before us, they are this generation and God has a plan through the dreams that he is releasing to them, for if their generation doesn't impart their wisdom of how God speaks with them through dreams, we will lose a significant part of who we are through the experiences that God has released upon them in their lifetime. The revelation in this teaching is great for you as well, as you begin to discern your dreams and visions through the word of God, God will begin to open your eyes to a deeper revelation of who you are in the Kingdom of God. When you take God seriously and you diligently seek him, he will release more of his talents upon you; the fruit in your life will begin to be poured out in an abundance of blessings from God like you have never seen before. I ask you are you up for the journey? I can assure you that a journey with God as your navigator is the best course to be on, so grab your bible, and get ready for an adventure with God. The next group of people that I would like to address is our children they are the next generation, if we don't impart the wisdom that God has revealed to us to our children, how will they know who God is. Children are able to discern dreams and visions by reading this book. My own children have a copy and they know how to break down a dream they have memorized what the symbols mean according to the word of God and they are able to discern their dreams as they are having them because children are like sponges they absorb everything that they find interesting. Let me tell you this, God is interesting to children take time to share who God is in your life, read the bible with your children. Spend time with your children asking them if they have had a dream lately. Show you are interested in their life by listening to them as they speak about their dreams or even nightmares that they may have, grab a spiral notebook and a pen writing down what they say, your children will see that you are truly interested in their life as you help them write down their dreams. When your children see that they have your undivided attention and you have paper and pen ready to write down what they say, there will be an outpouring from God that will flow from their lips directly to that piece of paper and you will not only be amazed at what God is revealing to your children, you may even experience a deeper revelation of who you are by how God speaks with your children. As you build a closer relationship with your children they will begin to tell you about their dreams or visions that they are having. Always make time to listen and never ever laugh at them or discredit what they are saying to you. Let them know that you can hardly wait to hear what they need to tell you, find a quiet place to share knowledge with each other. As I began to write down what God was sharing with my children, my eyes were opened to more revelation knowledge of who God is in all of our lives. I share this with you because it is so important that we teach our children how to understand who God is by releasing what they see in a dream. Children are pure in heart and God will impart his revelation knowledge over them I have seen this in my own children over and over again. I have included an interview with my 10 year old son Andrew of his dream of Hell and his dream of Heaven. When our children are taught to walk in the love of God and share what God gives them they walk in the love of God. I share my dreams and visions with my children and they have a deeper revelation of who God has called me to be and this helps them to understand who they are.

As I am breathing just as you breathe, I want you to know this Jesus is real. If you have ever doubted the reality of Jesus, please know that I would not tell you about this encounter with Jesus if it were not so. The word of God is infallible, and the truth of this encounter is that Jesus loves you. Jesus knew that I would write this to you, for this is the mantle that Jesus chose for me to embrace and decree over you, "Prepare the way of the Lord." Ever since this encounter there has been a passion that has not stopped burning within me, please take me seriously the Son of God is coming back for his bride, the bride needs to prepare herself for that wedding feast. Jesus is the King of Kings and Lord of Lords and one day every knee shall bow and every tongue will confess that Jesus is Lord! Glory to God in the highest!

INTRODUCTION

I am grateful to Apostle's Steven and Valerie Swisher who have always been there for me, they have allowed the gifts that God has placed upon my life to be imparted into the lives of others. God sure knew what he was doing when he placed me in this great house. Living Word Revival Center is a training center for Apostles, Prophets, Evangelists, Pastors and Teachers, where you will also see and feel the manifestation of God's presence operating in signs, miracles and wonders. As I have been on this journey with God, I have seen how God has taken everything he has placed upon my life and taken me in a complete circle of his love, just for me, to see who he truly is. The numerous dreams that continue to flow, endless hours of studying God's word for discernment of these dreams, studying the prophets in the bible to see if this is who I am and then God released the seer anointing; stepping out in faith in front of my church family and singing the song of the Lord over many different people, man that takes faith that only God can give. When you are truly committed to God, you only care about what God thinks knowing that he is with you he will not let you fail. There have been times I just heard one word and I knew that God would fill my mouth with his words by just stepping out and having that faith. Then, there are my awesome alone times with God, man I never feel I can ever have enough time with God. I can't wait to get to Heaven to bask in his beautiful splendor, with an exuberance of his joy emanating continually through my spirit, I open my eyes and see this world that God has created for me to live in, and I know that Heaven will be similar to this world, but there will be no evil only a fulfilling love that only our Lord can bring to us. I know that Heaven is a real place that God has made for his children, to enjoy for eternity. God has released so many songs over my life I am humbled at his love for me. He sings over me and I sing over him, a friendship that is comparable to none. Plain and simple God loves me for me, and I love God for God, for it is not what God can give me, it is who God is to me, God gave his only son Jesus Christ so that I would have a choice to choose eternal life in Heaven or eternal damnation in Hell. God is my best friend, I love him, I trust him and I can talk with him about anything and he always answers. The journey is still going, there are more dreams and visions to release, there is prophecy to fulfill over the lives of my brothers and sisters in Christ and those who have yet to know who my best friend is. As I am writing this to you, I am going to share with you a song that I sing to God that I guess you could say is our song. Every time I serenade God with our song I feel his breath close to me, I feel his heart beating in time with mine, but most of all, I feel his love. I pray that you will get to know God more by my experiences that I have had in my life. I wouldn't have missed God in this life for the world. God is the way, the truth and the life. Enjoy our song; the download is included with this book along with some of the other songs that are important for you to hear from God at this hour for we are truly walking in the latter days. God bless you.

FOREVER AND EVER AND EVER (SEPTEMBER 18, 2010)

Forever and ever and ever
I will call you my friend
Well your love, is amazing Lord
I will trust in you

Just to be with you,
My love, forever
Just to be with you,
Is where I love to be

And in your arms is where I love to be
You are holding me faithfully, forever
And in your arms is where I love to be
You are holding me faithfully, forever

Forever and ever and ever
I will call you my friend
Well your love is amazing Lord
I will trust in you

Just to be with you,
My love, forever
Just to be with you,
Is where, I love to be

And in your arms is where I love to be
You are holding me faithfully, forever
And in your arms is where I love to be
You are holding me faithfully, forever

And in your arms is where I love to be
You are holding me faithfully,
Faithfully…yours…

THE GATES OF HEAVEN

We are going to start with how God speaks with us. God
diversifies the way he speaks with us, he will speak through people,
through our circumstances, through an animal, a license plate, the
time, the seasons, a billboard, songs, smells, tastes, basically God
will use anything and everything to speak with us. Notice how I
said with us. When you speak to someone they don't listen, but
when you speak with someone they will listen. This is because
God knows us; he knows how to get our attention. I am going
to explain how God releases his wisdom to me. I will teach you
how to understand how God speaks through *all* of our senses. As
I began to write this morning, I asked the Lord, *Where do I begin
Lord?* This is what I heard, the music for the song "Love Story"
begins to play in my head and I begin to write, *Where do I begin,
to tell the story of how great a love can be, the sweet "Love Story" that
is older than the sea, the simple truth about the love he brings to me,
where do I start?* Now I am laughing and I feel the presence of
the Lord all around me. He is smiling, happy telling me just tell
everyone how much I love you. Also, tell them how much I love
them, for everything that I have bestowed upon you my love, is
also for them. At this point, I have tears of joy, knowing that God
will never leave me or forsake me, and the "Love Story" begins...
In the beginning of 2001, I had my first miscarriage. Losing that
baby was devastating, and so I began to blame God because my
baby died. Four months had passed and I became pregnant again,

two months into the pregnancy my baby died. I was so angry
with God for the loss of those babies. I shut the door to my
heart and mind of who God was to me. I wouldn't go to church,
I found myself blaming God all of the time for the loss of those
two children. This is a true account of meeting Jesus face to face,
in the summer of 2001.

One beautiful sunny morning the birds were singing my life
was still in grief, I was walking from my bedroom into the living
room when I felt the presence of someone staring at me to my
right. I stopped and turned to my right and was face to face with
Jesus. I was immediately drawn to tears rolling down his cheeks,
oh the shame I felt, for I had grieved Jesus, the son of God, the
one who shed his blood for me on Calvary. When Jesus spoke
his mouth did not move, every thought was revealed through
our minds. I stood in awe unable to move, with tears running
down my face. Then I asked, *"Why are you on the outside of my doors
Jesus?"* Then Jesus said, *"I am not to blame, your children are safe
inside the gates of Heaven, now come and let me in. Behold, I come to
save you for I am not to blame, your children are safe in Heaven one
day you three shall meet."* I asked Jesus to forgive me and he did
just like that. Jesus told me to write a song about this experience
and he also said that when I would sing it, that I was not to cry,
and that many people would come to the Kingdom of God from
this testimony. So, the song "The Gates of Heaven" is to glorify
who Jesus is and to bring his children safely back home inside
"The Gates of Heaven." Listen to the "The Gates of Heaven" that
is included as a download with this book, sit back close your eyes
and let the sound of Heaven invade Earth.

"THE GATES OF HEAVEN"

As I walk through the gates of Heaven
I see the Lamb of God
With his arms stretched open wide
I run to meet my savior
Welcome home my faithful friend,
In you I am well pleased,
The smile upon his face shouted sweet victory
The angels rejoice with me, singing

(Chorus with angels)
Holy, Holy, Holy
Holy is the lamb
Holy, Holy, Holy
Holy is the lamb

As I walk down the streets of gold
I look up to see the faces
Of the children I though lost to me
The smiles upon their faces, shouted sweet victory
The angels rejoice with me, singing

(Chorus with angels)
Holy, Holy, Holy
Holy is the lamb
Holy, Holy, Holy
Holy is the lamb

As I run through the streets of Heaven
I see a great mansion for me
I run through the doors and before me
Stand my friends and family
The smiles upon their faces, shouted sweet victory
The angels rejoice with me, singing

(Chorus with angels)
Holy, Holy, Holy
Holy is the lamb
Holy, Holy, Holy
Holy is the lamb
You are Holy, Oh so Holy, You are Holy
(Sherry A. Conrad, March 10, 2008)

After this experience, I had many questions for God. First I asked God, *"Why me God?" "Why would you take time for me, why am I so important to you?"* God's response, *"Because I love you more than you can even imagine."* I am always seeking after God and here are some scripture's that God enlightened me with so I could understand his heart for me. God states: *"As many as I love, I rebuke and chasten: Be zealous therefore and repent."*[11] Also, why was Jesus standing at the doors of my house? God states: *"Behold I stand at the door and knock: if any man hear my voice, and open the door, I will come in to him, and he with me. To him that overcometh will I grant him to sit with me in my throne, even as I overcame, and am set down with my Father in his throne. He that hath an ear let him hear what the Spirit saith unto the churches."*[12]

Here are some of the questions that people have asked me in reference to this visitation.

What was Jesus wearing?
Jesus was wearing a white linen gown with long sleeves I did not see his feet.

What color is Jesus' hair?
His hair is a golden brown.

What color were his eyes?
His eyes are blue, as blue as the deep blue sea.

What do you mean he spoke to you through your mind?
Even before I could begin to ask, Jesus already knew what I was going to ask. *"And the Spirit of the Lord fell upon me, and said unto me, speak; Thus saith the Lord; O house of Israel: for I know the things that come into your mind, every one of them."*[13]

It took 7 years to begin to share my experience of meeting Jesus face to face. I finally sat down March 10, 2008 to write "The Gates of Heaven." That had to be the hardest day and yet the most beneficial day of my life because finally, I was able to cry out all of the tears that had been bottled up inside of me for 7 years. As I wrote the words just flowed from the pen onto the paper, with my tears saturating every word. This was the beginning of the Psalmist anointing that Jesus prophesied over me the day I met him face to face. Stop for a minute, close your eyes and let the vision of how Jesus spoke with me open your eyes, ears and heart to hear what he is speaking to you today. This was not just for me, this is for all to hear and learn from. Now, let's talk about keeping a dream journal. We are also going to talk about keeping a notepad with you at all times that will fit into your purse or your pocket and make sure that you always have a pen to write with. God will speak with you not only through dreams; he will also speak with you during the day through visions. I never know when God is going to show me a vision so I am always expecting to see or hear a new revelation from God. We are also going to discern some of these visions that God has given to me. This will help you with your journey along the way. There is one more very important fact to point out. Does Satan know what the call on your life is? You bet he does. In the summer of 2011, I had an encounter with one of Satan's pawns, a "sweet little old lady" that knew things about my life from the time I was a little girl. She told me about the encounter that I had with Jesus and told me that I had to make a very important decision. Remember, I did not know this woman at all. I sang the "Gates of Heaven" for her and she told me that song was just for me and no one else. Jesus told me to write this, and I have sung this song several times over different people and the anointing of God was all over this as the song of the Lord was released. Remember this not everyone you meet has the heart of God within them, they may look like they do on the outside, but the Lord said this to Samuel, *"Do not look on his appearance or on the height of his stature, because I have rejected him. For the Lord sees not as man sees; man looks on the outward appearance, but the Lord looks on the heart.*[14] *Beware of false prophets, which come to you in sheep's clothing, but inwardly they are ravening wolves."*[15]

THE DREAM/VISION JOURNAL

I would recommend that you get a 2-inch, 3 ring binder, that has a plastic sleeve cover on the front, a spiral notebook, and that you make a typed copy of "The Discernment of a Dream/Vision" list of questions and place them in your binder. You will find this list within this chapter. Including this page with questions will help you to discern your dream/vision. You can also include a pen/pencil pouch that you can keep all of your supplies in. Make a cover page to slip into the front of the binder that says, "The Dream/Vision Journal." Keep your spiral notebook from your dream/vision journal by your bed on your nightstand or under your pillow with a pen ready to write. There are also pens that light up so that you can write with a light in the middle of the night. I also keep a book light handy and another great tool to invest in is a mini hand held recorder that you can speak your dream into and then listen to it later to reveal the revelation. Personally, I have one to sing songs into when God releases them to me as well, this way I have the words and the melody so I will not forget. I have been awakened in the middle of the night to write down a dream that God has revealed. Also, sometimes you will draw a picture of what you saw in the dream, or find a picture of what you saw. This will help you to find the relevance of the dream. There have been times when God has revealed more of a vision during the day that I did dream about either the night before or at some other time, so I would recommend that you carry a small notepad with you and pen to jot these memories down. If you carry an electronic device with you, you can add it to your notepad there or you can record the information as well. A most important fact to see and hear is this: God will speak to you with pictures, words, sounds, smells, tastes, numbers & colors that you will understand. You are probably thinking why should I go to all of this trouble to set up my journal, why can't I just use a spiral notebook? You can but later on I am talking about in a year from now, when you start to put all of your dreams together it is much easier to have them broken down in this format instead of scrambling to find which notebook you wrote a dream in. If you keep it all together along with all of your research God will see that you are taking him seriously and will begin to reveal more to you. This is what I have seen throughout my life with God that he will reveal more of his heart to me, the more I seek him the more I find him. God uses experiences that you have encountered in your life; this is so you will be able to discern what God is relaying to you. When discerning a dream, God is always the best source to go to for he knows you best! The more time you spend studying God's word, God says he will reveal revelation knowledge. God states that: *"For there is nothing hidden except to be revealed, nor is anything kept secret except in order that it may be known."*[16] If there is part of the dream that you do not understand, fast and pray about it. God's timing is always perfect.

As a reference to help you to discern a dream, I would also recommend, the Holy Bible, Strong's expanded exhaustive concordance of the bible the encyclopedia, the dictionary and the thesaurus. Over the years, I have learned that God will use people I know because of what their names mean. You can search the internet on a baby names site for the information that you are looking for; also you can search a name for the Hebrew aphorism. It is very pertinent that you seek God's heart and the Holy Spirit that lives within you will confirm the meaning of the name. At the back of this book is an extensive dream/vision symbolic dictionary with reference to scripture as well as some of my personal experiences with a particular symbol that pertained to me in my life. Please understand that God will speak with you in reference to symbols that you will relate with, there is no way possible for me to include everything that God will show you. Know this that God created everything in this world, so research the facts about what God has shown you. For example, if God were to show you a *rabbit* in a dream research about the *rabbit* and why God showed the *rabbit* to you. The *rabbit* represents multiplication because of the *rabbit's* gregarious character they attract many people and people will want to be around them to listen to what they have to say. A *rabbit* also burrow's meaning they are able to find shelter and comfort in God. They have long ears, meaning they are able to hear what God is saying and release his word. Their long legs mean they can jump high and run very fast, meaning the ministry that they have will spread rapidly throughout the nations. A *rabbit* can also be linked to a new ministry that God has placed in your life. So, understand just because the world says that the *rabbit* died it is not literal to death or pregnancy. Years ago the urine of a pregnant woman would be injected into a *rabbit* and they would kill the *rabbit* to observe the ovaries of the rabbit, if the ovaries had bulging masses growing on their ovaries, this would mean that the woman was pregnant. So, the *rabbit* always had to die years ago to find out if a woman was pregnant. There are many ways that God will relay messages to you through dreams, I have been awakened in the night on several occasions with a choir of angels singing! The first time this happened, the angels kept singing until I finally got up out of bed and wrote down all of

the words and sang the melody on my recorder. Then I was able
to go back to sleep!

THE DISCERNMENT OF A DREAM/VISION

Use this as a guideline as you are writing in your dream/vision
journal. Every detail is important for you to write down as you are
interpreting what you have seen. Always keep your journals and
from time to time, go back to them you will begin to see what God
is doing in your life! I have spent many hours compiling a dream/
vision dictionary of symbols in the back of this book. Remember,
that God will show you symbols that you will understand, they
will be experiences that have happened to you in your life that
only you and God know about. It is also important to point out
that we need to use the word of God for discernment. There will
be times that you will need to fast and pray about a dream/vision.
After the discernment of a dream/vision, I will add a title to show
importance of the revelation of what it is that God is showing
to me.

Title of dream/vision:

_____

What happened in the dream/vision?

_____
_____
_____
_____
_____
_____

Who is in your dream/vision?

_____

_____

_____

_____

Where are you in the dream/vision?

_____

_____

_____

When did this happen in the dream/vision?

_____

_____

_____

Why did this happen in the dream/vision?

_____

_____

_____

What objects/colors are highlighted in this dream/vision?

_____

_____

_____

What is God saying to you in this dream/vision? The discernment here is to diligently seek God he is taking you on a journey so that you will learn more about who he is to you, and who you are to him.

_____

_____

_____

_____

_____

_____

The more you know God, the more God will release to you. Diligently seek God's heart asking him for wisdom. There will be times that you will not fully understand everything that you see, however, God will release his revelation knowledge of what he has shown you so that you will come to an understanding. Some dreams/visions are easier to discern than others are this is completely normal. Please do not get frustrated and give up in God's perfect time you will understand.

Since my childhood, I have experienced dreams and visions. As a child though I never fully understood what they meant. Through the years, I have been seeking God diligently for answers about this. You see I would share a dream with a friend and they could not understand because they did not dream. I have been laughed at, and this hurt deep inside, I wanted so much to be able to relate to other people to share my feelings with them about this. So, what happened? God became my closest friend! God speaks with us through music as well. One morning, when I woke up, I heard the song "You've got a friend" by James Taylor playing in the Spirit from God. I have to laugh because God is always thinking of ways to catch my attention. So, I got out of bed went to my computer and listened to the song over the internet. Wow, what a powerful message God was relaying to me at this moment.

Isn't God awesome, I know I'm not the only one that God talks with. Whenever I hear this song on the radio, immediately the peace of God just comes over me. One day recently the kids were yelling and screaming, we got into the van as soon as I started the van I heard this song, the peace of God just filled the atmosphere. God wants us to know that he is with us always, believe it because he is!!! I am a friend of God just like Abraham, *"And the scripture was fulfilled which saith, Abraham believed God, and it was imputed unto him for righteousness: and he was called the Friend of God.*"[17] God really loves us so much that he will manifest his presence so we will be able to smell his presence. One night my children and I attended a home group meeting; we all had dinner together and worshipped the Lord. Then we spoke about what the Lord is doing in this hour. As different people began to share revelation knowledge from the Lord I smelled a really strong scent like I have never smelled before. There were so many different kinds of flowers awakening my senses all at once. I turned to my friend and said do you smell that she smiled and said yes. Then I asked my son Andrew and daughter Christina and they said they smelled it too. Then I asked another friend and he said he thought it was something that the kids had, not realizing that it wasn't. I have *never* smelled this before, and with *such intensity*! So, when I got home I started to seek the Lord for his knowledge about this and this is what I have found out. *"Now thanks be unto God, which always causeth us to triumph in Christ, and maketh manifest the savour of his knowledge by us in every place."*[18] When I read this scripture I knew immediately that this is a sign of revelation knowledge from the Lord. The fragrance of the Lord was indeed in our presence and I knew his holy spirit was filling me and guiding my way. The fragrance of God is a confirmation from God for his love for us, walking in faith by allowing God to lead our way. I know that because of my choice to be a devoted servant and because of my commitment and obedience, the Lord was pleased and was rewarding me. Hence, *"But without faith it is impossible to please Him, for he who come to God must believe that He is, and that He is a rewarder of them who diligently seek him."*[19] I thank you Lord for revealing the sweet fragrance of your presence, I thank you for filling me with more of you, until I am so full of you Lord that people will no longer see me. "All of you Lord and none of me," is what I strive for in my life. For I have come to see that when we allow God's spirit to flow through us, Heaven invades this Earth that we live in and miracles, signs and wonders begin to manifest all around us. God is opening up the flood gates of Heaven upon his children, all we need to do to receive is to walk in that spiritual oneness with God. Listening for God's voice emanating through the darkness that lights up the entire atmosphere releasing God's glory upon this Earth. Putting off our fleshly thinking and putting on the mind of Christ, worshipping God in spirit and truth. Thank you Lord for you are a great Father who rewards his children with good gifts that only you can give. Thank you for my salvation, for that my Lord is your greatest gift of all, *love*.

WHAT IS A DREAM AND A VISION?

A *dream* is a series of thoughts, images, or emotions occurring during sleep.[20] Our dreams are either released by God or Satan. There are many examples of dreams in the bible; here are two that will help you grasp a better understanding of what a dream is.

"Thou, O king, sawest, and behold a great image. This great image, whose brightness was excellent, stood before thee; and the form thereof was terrible. This image's head was of fine gold, his breast and his arms of silver, his belly and his thighs of brass. His legs of iron, his feet part of iron and part of clay. Thou sawest till that a stone was cut out without hands, which smote the image upon his feet that were of iron and clay, and brake them to pieces. Then was the iron, the clay, the brass, the silver, and the gold, broken to pieces together, and became like chaff of the summer threshingfloors; and the wind carried them away, that no place was found for them: and the stone that smote the image became a great mountain, and filled the whole earth."[21]

And Jacob went out from Beersheba, and went toward Haran. And he lighted upon a certain place, and tarried there all night, because the sun was set; and he took of the stones of that place, and put them for his pillows, and lay down in that place to sleep. And he dreamed, and behold a ladder set up on the earth, and the top of it reached to heaven: and behold the angels of God ascending and descending on it. And, behold, the Lord stood above it, and said, *"I am the Lord God of Abraham thy father, and the God of Isaac: the land whereon thou liest, to thee will I give it, and to thy seed; And thy seed shall be as the dust of the earth, and thou shalt spread abroad to the west, and to the east, and to the north, and to the south: and in thee in thy seed shall all the families of the earth be blessed. And, behold I am with thee, and will keep thee in all places whither thou goest, and will bring thee again into this land; for I will not leave thee, until I have done that which I have spoken to thee of."[22]*

Many people have asked if Satan can attack us while we are asleep, think on this Satan attacks while you are awake. The answer is yes, this is why it is so important to pray before going to sleep, and it is also important to know how to pray if the enemy attacks you during your sleep. If this ever happens to you take authority over the situation that is happening in your dream, say this with authority, with boldness, *"In the name of Jesus I command*

you to go!!!" When you take authority over the situation Satan has to go. *There is no other name like Jesus and Satan knows this.*

The definition of *vision* is unusual wisdom in foreseeing what is going to happen.[23] *Visions* are seen while you are awake that is the difference between a *dream* and a *vision*. Our *visions* are either released by God or by Satan. There are many examples of visions in the bible; here are two that will help you grasp a better understanding of what a vision is.

And as they thus spake, Jesus himself stood in the midst of them, and saith unto them, *"Peace be unto you."* But they were terrified and affrighted, and supposed that they had seen a spirit. And he said unto them, *"Why are ye troubled? And why do thoughts arise in your hearts? Behold my hands and my feet, that it is I myself: handle me, and see; for a spirit hath not flesh and bones, as ye see me have."* And when he had thus spoken, he shewed them his hands and his feet. And while they yet believed not for joy, and wondered, he said unto them, *"Have ye here any meat?"* And they gave him a piece of broiled fish, and of an honeycomb. And he took it, and did eat before them.[24]

And after six days Jesus taketh Peter, James, and John his brother, and bringeth them up into an high mountain apart. And was transfigured before them: and his face did shine as the sun, and his raiment was white as the light. And, behold, there appeared unto them Moses and Elias as talking with him. Then answered Peter, and said unto Jesus, *"Lord, it is good for us to be here: if thou wilt, let us make here three tabernacles: one for thee, and one for Moses, and one for Elias."* While he yet spake, behold, a bright cloud overshadowed them: and behold a voice out of the cloud, which said, *"This is my beloved Son, in whom I am well-pleased; hear ye him."* And when the disciples heard it, they fell on their face, and were sore afraid. And Jesus came and touched them, and said, *"Arise and be not afraid."* And when they had lifted up their eyes, they saw no man, save Jesus only. And as they came down from the mountain, Jesus charged them, saying, *"Tell the vision to no man, until the Son of man be risen again from the dead."* And the disciples asked him, saying, *"Why then say the scribes that Elias must first come?"* And Jesus answered and said unto them, *"Elias is come already, and they knew him not, but have done unto him whatsoever they listed, likewise shall also the Son of man suffer of them."* Then the disciples understood that he spake unto them of John the Baptist.[25]

A PARABLE IS A DREAM OR VISION.

Jesus taught in parables, which is a simple story used to illustrate a moral or spiritual lesson. During his teaching, Jesus would assimilate objects within our life as a figure of speech like a metaphor. A metaphor is a figure of speech in which a word for one idea or thing is used in place of another to suggest a likeness between them (as in "the ship plows the sea").[26] Allegorically speaking a parable is a simple story told to illustrate a moral truth.[27] Let's look at a teaching parable given by Jesus Christ; And he began again to teach by the sea side: and there was gathered unto him a great multitude, so that he entered into a ship, and sat in the sea; and the whole multitude was by the sea on the land. And he taught them many things by parables, and said unto them in his doctrine, *"Hearken; Behold, there went out a sower to sow: And it came to pass, as he sowed, some fell by the way side, and the fowls of the air came and devoured it up. And some fell on stony ground, where it had not much earth; and immediately it sprang up, because it had no depth of earth: But when the sun was up, it was scorched; and because it had no root, it withered away. And some fell among thorns, and the thorns grew up, and choked it, and it yielded no fruit. And other fell on good ground, and did yield fruit that sprang up and increased; and brought forth, some thirty, and some sixty, and some an hundred."* And he said unto them, *"He that hath ears to hear, let him hear."* And when he was alone, they that were about him with the twelve asked of him the parable. And he said unto them, *"Unto you it is given to know the mystery of the kingdom of God: but unto them that are without, all these things are done in parables: That seeing they may see, and not perceive; and hearing they may hear, and not understand; lest at any time they should be converted, and their sins should be forgiven them."* And he said unto them, *"Know ye not this parable? And how then will ye know all parables? The sower soweth the word. And these are they by the way side, where the word is sown; but when they have heard, Satan cometh immediately, and taketh away the word that was sown in their hearts. And these are they likewise which are sown on stony ground; who, when they have heard the word, immediately receive it with gladness; And have no root in themselves, and so endure but for a time: afterward, when affliction or persecution ariseth for the word's sake, immediately they are offended. And these are they which are sown among thorns; such as hear the word, And the cares of this world, and the deceitfulness of riches, and the lusts of other things entering in, choke the word, and it becometh unfruitful. And these are they which are sown on good ground; such as hear the word, and receive it, and bring forth fruit, some thirtyfold, some sixty, and some an hundred."* And he said unto them, *"Is a candle brought to be put under a bushel, or under a bed? and not to be set on a candlestick? For there is nothing hid, which shall not be manifested; neither was any thing kept secret, but that it should come abroad. If any man have ears to hear, let him hear."* And he said unto them, *"Take heed what ye hear: with what measure ye mete, it shall be measured to you: and unto you that hear shall more be given. For he that hath, to him shall be given: and he that hath not, from him shall be taken even that which he hath."* And he said, *"So is the kingdom of God, as if a man should cast seed into the ground; And should sleep, and rise night and day, and the seed should spring and grow up, he knoweth not how. For the earth bringeth forth fruit of herself; first the blade, then the ear, after that the full corn in the ear. But when the fruit is brought forth, immediately he putteth in the sickle, because the harvest is come."* And he said, *"Whereunto shall we liken the kingdom of God? Or with what comparison shall we compare it? It is like a grain of mustard seed, which, when it is sown in the earth, is less than all the seeds that be in the earth: But when it is sown, it groweth up, and becometh greater than all herbs, and shooteth out great branches; so that the fowls of the air may lodge under the shadow of it."* And with many such parables spake he the word unto them, as they were able to hear it. But without a parable spake he not unto them: and when they were alone, he expounded all things to his disciples.[28]

Jesus had a relationship with the twelve disciples, and when Jesus was alone with the twelve disciples, Jesus would explain in detail the meaning of the parables that he would teach amongst the multitudes of people. Why didn't Jesus explain to the multitude of people the in depth meaning of the parables that he taught on? Jesus said to his disciples, *"Unto you it is given to know the mystery of the kingdom of God: but unto them that are without, all these things are done in parables: That seeing they may see, and not perceive; and hearing they may hear, and not understand; lest at any time they* *should be converted, and their sins should be forgiven them."*²⁹ Jesus said to the disciples, that they were given to know the mystery of the kingdom of God because they knew who God was and they would understand as Jesus explained the parable, the disciples, could see God, and hear God they completely understood God because they had a relationship with God. However, the people who did not know God would only be spoken to in parables because they could not see God, they could not hear what God was saying to them, and they could not understand God. The people that did not know God were fearful that they may be changed and that they could no longer be in their sin. Jesus also said, *"Therefore speak I to them in parables: because they seeing see not; and hearing they hear not, neither do they understand. And in them is fulfilled the prophecy of Esaias, which saith, By hearing ye shall hear, and shall not understand; and seeing ye shall see, and shall not perceive: For this people's heart is waxed gross, and their ears are dull of hearing, and their eyes they have closed; lest at any time they should see with their eyes, and hear with their ears, and should understand with their heart, and should be converted, and I should heal them."*³⁰ The key to unlocking the mystery of the Kingdom of God is to have a relationship with him. God created you in his image to walk with you and talk with you along the way. God loves you; God needs you he only wants to be with you. It is God's will to spend eternity with you in Heaven forevermore. Feel the rain of the Holy Spirit saturating you as God pours down his tears from Heaven over you. Listen to *"Tears from Heaven"* closing your eyes focusing on this message from God and let God draw you closer to his heart revealing to you who he is. He is the great *I Am, the Alpha and the Omega, God is love.*

LITTLE BO PEEP
(THE CALL TO MINISTRY)

When I opened my eyes, I was wearing a dress just like *Little Bo Peep* wears in one of my favorite children's movies. *(God will use experiences that you have had in your life, this is so you will be able to discern what God is relaying to you).* I saw the full white bottom of the dress with pink polka dots and then I heard my earthly father's voice speak these words: *"Feed my sheep!"* As he spoke these words to me, he stretched forth a beautiful wooden hand carved staff, I grabbed the staff with my right hand. I focused on the dogwood flower that was so meticulously engraved into the handle of the staff. Upon the staff was also the engraving of leaves of the tree of the dogwood tree. This staff was exquisite in detail. Then, I looked out to see where I was, and I was in this large football stadium that had no ceiling! It was nighttime and all the lights were on, I was standing in the seating area amongst the crowd, looking out upon thousands of people waiting for me to share the word of God.

BREAKING DOWN THE DREAM: LITTLE BO PEEP

Who is *Little Bo Peep* to me?

_____

_____

_____

_____

Why do I hear my earthly father's voice?

_____

_____

_____

_____

Why did I grab the wooden staff placed with my right hand?

_____

_____

_____

_____

Why would God have me focus on the engraved dogwood flower?

_____

_____

_____

_____

Why am I at a football stadium with no ceiling, dressed like *Little Bo Peep?*

_____

_____

_____

_____

REVELATION OF BREAKING DOWN THE DREAM: LITTLE BO PEEP

Who is *Little Bo Peep* to me?

Little Bo Peep is a shepherd, she guards the sheep. God is showing me *Little Bo Peep*, she is one of my favorite characters. God loves to show us pictures that we will relate to! God has *called me to Pastor his children.*

Why do I hear my earthly father's voice?

I respect and listen to my earthly father that God has placed within my life. When I hear my earthly father's voice speak I am listening and receiving the revelation of God my Father. *"My sheep hear my voice, and I know them, and they follow me."*[31] I would like to point out, at this moment in my walk with God I was just learning to hear God's voice, God knew that I would listen to my earthly father's voice.

Why did I grab the wooden staff with my right hand?

I grabbed the wooden staff with my right hand accepting the position of authority that I have with God here on this Earth. *"Who is gone into heaven, and is on the right hand of God: angels and authorities and powers being made subject unto him."*[32] This is the call that God has placed upon my life, to deliver his word to his children, God has called me to *Pastor* his children. Being the light in the darkness, this is why it is nighttime in my dream and you see all of the lights on revealing not only who I am in Christ, but also where I am to speak the word of God. You see God is always watching over his children, even when they are not walking with him he is looking for that one lost child.

Why would God have me focus on the engraved dogwood flower?

Jesus is a carpenter, the engraved dogwood flower, signifies new beginnings. *"Is not this the carpenter, the son of Mary, the brother of James, and Joses, and of Juda, and Simon? And are not his sisters here with us? And they were offended at him."*[33] As I studied the word of God about the staff this is what I have found out. The rod of Aaron once sprouted overnight with a living branch containing leaves and ripe almonds. And it came to pass, that on the morrow Moses went into the tabernacle of witness; and, behold, the rod of Aaron for the house of Levi was budded, and brought forth buds, and bloomed blossoms, and yielded almonds. And Moses brought out all the rods from before the Lord unto all the children of Israel: and they looked, and took every man his rod. And the Lord said unto Moses, *"Bring Aaron's rod again before the testimony, to be kept for a token against the rebels; and thou shalt quite take away their murmurings from me, that they die not."*[34] This happened when the staff was placed before the Ark in the Tabernacle. God used this miraculous sign to show the Israelites that he fully approved the choice of Aaron and his Levite clan to regain priesthood. There are many references in the word of God that the rod is the rod of God. Let see, And Moses took his wife and his sons, and set them upon an ass, and he returned to the land of Egypt: and Moses took the rod of God in his hand.[35] Also, And Moses said unto Joshua, *"Choose us out men, and go out, fight with Amalek: tomorrow I will stand on the top of the hill with the rod of God in mine hand."*[36] Allegorically, it also signifies the high priesthood of Christ, our authority through Christ in this world to walk in the love of Jesus Christ sharing God's word with his children. I can draw all men near with the rod of God for he has given me the authority to do so.

Why am I at a football stadium with no ceiling, dressed like *Little Bo Peep?*

Now in reality, this would be really funny if I went to a football game dressed like this, for those who know me I would wear that if God told me to because I am walking in obedience with what God tells me to do, not what man expects me to do. God is showing me who I am. I am a shepherd sharing God's word with his children, and by stepping out into the calling that God has for my life, many will come to know who God is. A football stadium holds approximately 100,000 people; *wow* that's a lot of people![37] It is also important to point out here that I saw no ceiling where I was in this football stadium when you are walking in God's will there is no ceiling God continues to take you from glory to glory.

This dream means that God is calling me to *Pastor* his children, and the journey begins...

God's timing is perfect and God could have waited another 10 or 20 more years to release this information. I have gathered all of the dreams that God has given to me over the years and what revelation! I have studied God's word and prayed for his insight. I have fasted as Daniel fasted to receive revelation from God. Wait upon the Lord and he will reveal the dreams that he bestows upon you. Through this journey, (as I am holding back tears), I have truly come to *know God, he is my Father and I can trust him like I have never trusted anyone before in my life.* God will open our eyes to see in a dream…now we will trust in God to walk out what we have seen by faith in God! Let our faith increase in you God. Oh, the many aspects of God, I just love him so much. He makes me laugh, cry, jump for joy, scream out loud, sing for him knowing that he is there comforting me along the way.

As I have walked through this journey, I have learned to hear God's voice. The more I have come to know God, the more God has released to me in dreams. In the beginning, I would see and hear. Then, I began to be able to feel, taste and smell as well. God will awaken all of your senses the closer you come to know him. There are some dreams that are just for you that only you need to know. People will become jealous or not believe you and this is *not* good because this can lead to a drawing away from God. In the bible we are told we are peculiar people, I don't know about you but I don't want to be ordinary I want to be peculiar. *"But ye are a chosen generation, a royal priesthood, an holy nation, a peculiar people; that ye should shew forth the praises of him who hath called you out of darkness into his marvellous light."*[38] Who will you trust? Trust in God, he is the one who is revealing his secrets to you.

MEDITATE ON THE WORD OF GOD

Mine eyes prevent the night watches, that I might meditate in thy word.[39]

Focus on this vision that God gave to Daniel; then write down the revelation you receive from God that pertains to your life. God will begin to open your eyes and ears in a new way. *"Behold, I will do a new thing; now it shall spring forth; shall ye not know it? I will even make a way in the wilderness, and rivers in the desert."*[40]

Begin to see and hear what God is saying, bringing insight to your life!

VISION OF THE LORD: DANIEL 10:5-6

Then I lifted up mine eyes, and looked, and behold a certain man clothed in linen, whose loins were girded with fine gold of Uphaz: His body was like beryl, and his face as the appearance of lightning, and his eyes lamps of fire, and his arms and his feet like in colour to polished brass, and the voice of a multitude. (While in prayer with God, God gave me this discernment to help me to understand how the appearance of his body looked to Daniel. Get some "bronzing lotion with shimmer" added to it and rub some into the back of your hand, and see how it shimmers in "the light" also notice the "bronze" color on your skin! Of course God's body shimmers for he is the "Father of Lights" with light permeating throughout his entire body!).

Reference these two scriptures to help you discern this vision:
"And I turned to see the voice that spake with me, And being turned, I saw seven golden candlesticks; And in the midst of the seven candlesticks one like unto the Son of man, clothed with a garment down to the foot, and girt about the paps with a golden girdle. His head and his hairs where white like wool, as white as snow; and his eyes were as a flame of fire. And his feet like unto fine brass, as if they burned in a furnace; and his voice as the sound of many waters. And he had in his right hand seven stars: and out of his mouth went a sharp two-edged sword: and his countenance was as the sun shineth in his strength."[41]

"And I heard as if were the voice of a great multitude, and as the voice of many waters, and as the voice of mighty thunderings, saying Aleluia: for the Lord God omnipotent reigneth."[42]

What is God saying to you about this vision?

_____

_____

_____

_____

I would like to share a vision with you that is similar to the vision that Daniel shared with us in (Daniel 10:5-6).

While worshipping the Lord one day this is the vision I saw: I saw a man with a very muscular body, his body was bronze, with a golden glow. His hair was white as snow, very long approximately to his lower back. He also had a mustache and long beard. In his right hand, he was holding a golden rod. His eyes were flames of fire and he was wearing blue pants. I just stayed in his presence and felt a peace and knew without doubt that this was God my Father. He didn't say anything he just stayed in front of my eyes as I worshipped him in all his glory!

The reason his pants are blue signify that we are to remember the commandments of the Lord, And the Lord spake unto Moses, saying, "*Speak unto the children of Israel, and bid them that they make them fringes in the borders of their garments throughout their generations, and that they put upon the fringe of the borders a ribband of blue: And it shall be unto you for a fringe, that ye may look upon it, and remember all the commandments of the Lord your God, which brought you out of the land of Egypt, to be your God: I am the Lord your God.*"[43]

God my Father just wanted to spend time with me, as I rest in the presence of God I am renewed in my strength. The Prophet Isaiah tells me, "*But they that wait upon the Lord shall renew their strength; they shall mount up with wings as eagles; they shall run, and not be weary; and they shall walk, and not faint.*"[44] I am able to continue to run the race, to stand in the storms that this world I live in throws my way. The Apostle Paul writes, "*And be not conformed to this world: but be ye transformed by the renewing of your mind, that ye may prove what is that good, and acceptable, and perfect, will of God.*"[45] Trust in God with your entire mind, taking captive every sinful thought as soon as it enters your mind. Always trusting in God he is your Father and he loves you, he is directing your path.

PRAISE AND WORSHIP THE LORD IN SPIRIT AND TRUTH!

God will begin to release dreams and visions within your life as you draw closer to him by praising and worshipping him in spirit and truth. I have seen this manifest in my own personal relationship with God, I make time for God *throughout each day* to praise and worship him. Notice how I stated *throughout each day*, you see God is my Father and I seek counsel with him every day throughout my day, I have learned this example from Jesus. Jesus always sought after the will of God and that is how we are supposed to live our lives as well. Someone once said to me that I have a stronger relationship with God because I have more time to spend with him. That statement in itself is ridiculous, we all have the same 24 hours in each day; you control how those hours are spent. As Ambassadors for the Kingdom of God we are called to a higher standard. Get up earlier or go to bed later, stop watching every show on television and playing every game that is on this planet. God created this Earth, and God is worthy of your time. The truth of that statement is that I do have a stronger relationship because I truly want to be with God, he is my Father, he is my friend, God means everything to me and I will praise and worship God in spirit and truth. Take counsel from Jesus as he describes how we are to worship God. Jesus said, *"But the hour cometh, and now is, when the true worshippers shall worship the Father in spirit and truth: for the Father seeketh such to worship him. God is a Spirit: and they that worship him must worship him in spirit and truth."*[46] Jesus tells us that the hour is now for the true worshippers to worship the Father in spirit and truth. We were made to worship God! This is our very nature for he is our creator and we are to praise and worship him always. Always thank God for the blessings that he has bestowed upon your life, for he alone is worthy, and every blessing comes from God alone. I have spoken with other people who declare over their lives that they never have a dream or vision that God does not speak with them in this way. Let me tell you my friend, this is a lie from Satan, and believe me Satan knows how to use the word of God to his advantage and twist God's word, for he tries to be like God. We are told in the book of Job, *"Thou shalt also decree a thing, and it shall be established unto thee: and the light shall shine upon thy ways."*[47] So, as we reference this we see that we are speaking an untruth into our lives, thus instead of the light of God shining upon our ways, the darkness of Satan is casting a shadow upon our eyes and covering our ears so that we can't see or hear what God is speaking. What we say and what we think affect our lives and the lives of other people. I can tell you this that I have decreed that a person would have a dream or vision from God and God always opens their eyes to see and they are truly amazed because they thought or spoke into their life that this was not possible, that God never speaks with them in this way. With God all things are possible! I decree over your life that any negative words or thoughts that you have spoken or thought over your dream or vision life are cut off in the name of Jesus. I decree that God is opening your eyes and ears to see and hear all that he has for you.

It is always important that you use the word of God in the bible to confirm a dream or vision of what God is relaying to you. It must be biblically sound. There are new age books about dreams and visions that will lead you astray. Just because the world says, "Wise as an owl" don't believe the world, where does this come from? This comes from the goddess of wisdom and she is depicted as an owl. Athene/Athena is the Greek goddess of wisdom, the Roman version of Minerva whose symbols are the owl, olive branch, and the snake.[48] There are people in our world today known as the Bohemians that worship a forty foot owl. To Bohemians, the owl has come to symbolize the wisdom of life and companionship that allows humans to struggle with and survive the cares and frustration of the world. A forty foot concrete (or stone, sources vary) owl stands at the head of the lake in the Grove. Built to serve as a ceremonial site for traditional Bohemian rituals, the Owl of Bohemia is used yearly for the Cremation of Care Ceremony.[49] This is in our world today, don't be blind to what is around you in the world fill yourself with the wisdom and knowledge that only God can reveal to you. *"Professing themselves to be wise, they became fools, and changed the glory of the uncorruptible God into and image made like to corruptible man, and to birds, and four-footed beasts, and creeping things."*[50]

FROZEN MEAT ON THE PRAYER SHAWL

This is a vision the Lord spoke to me, God said, "Take
four pieces of frozen steak, place them on the prayer shawl
out in the sun, now what does this mean to you?"

I prayed for God to release his wisdom to me, *"If any of you lack
wisdom, let him ask of God, that giveth to all men liberally, and
unbraideth not; and it shall be given him."*[51]

BREAKING DOWN THE VISION: FROZEN MEAT ON THE PRAYER SHAWL

What does the frozen meat represent?

_____

_____

_____

_____

What does the number 4 represent?

_____

_____

_____

_____

Why is the frozen meat placed on the prayer shawl?

_____

_____

_____

_____

REVELATION OF BREAKING DOWN THE VISION: FROZEN MEAT ON THE PRAYER SHAWL

What does the frozen meat represent?

The *frozen meat* symbolizes the people in this world who are *frozen in their flesh* to knowing *Jesus Christ*. People who are *frozen in their flesh* have either never heard the body of Christ preach the gospel of *Jesus Christ*. Or, they have heard who *Jesus Christ* is by the body of *Jesus Christ* and have decided by their own will not to follow Jesus. This is what God is saying; *"The body of Christ needs to be aware of his or her authority and step into the calling that I have placed upon their lives. The harvest is ready, the fields have been sown it is time to reap! Take your positions in the battlefield and know that the Lord your God is with you!"*

Stop right here and answer this question: Do you know what your position or positions are in *the body of Christ*? Who are you? For some of you God has already spoken with you about this and you are walking in the office that God has called you to. For others you are still pondering where to start, or waiting for another confirmation from God. Stop pondering who you are, take that step forward into the office that God has placed you in. For those of you who know who God has called you to be, but you are waiting for God to tell you again, *stop it!* God has already told you who you are why does he need to tell you again, move forward! Put a check by the office or office's that you believe that you are *called to walk in.* As you have just read the word that God has spoken to me to tell you, *"The body of Christ needs to be aware of his or her authority and step into the calling that I have placed upon their lives. The harvest if ready, the fields have been sown it is time to reap! Take your positions in the battlefield and know that the Lord your God is with you!"* Trust in God with all of your heart for he is faithful he will never leave you or forsake you.

1. Apostle _____   _____

An Apostle is a person who initiates or first advocates a great reform.[52]

2. Prophet/Seer _____

A Prophet/Seer is one who predicts future events or developments.[53]

3. Evangelist _____

The Evangelist is the writer of any of the four Gospels.[54] To be an Evangelist is to evangelize, meaning to preach the gospel and to convert to Christianity.[55] The gospel is the teachings of Christ and the apostles, any of the first four books of the New Testament, and something accepted or promoted as infallible truth.[56] The infallible truth is incapable of error.[57] Let's look at what the Apostle Peter told us about the infallible truth our Lord Jesus Christ, *"For we have not followed cunningly devised fables, when we made known unto you the power and coming of our Lord Jesus Christ, but were eyewitnesses of his majesty. For he received from God the Father honour and glory, when there came such a voice to him from the excellent glory, This is my beloved Son, in whom I am well pleased. And this voice which came from heaven we heard, when we were with him in the holy mount. We have also a more sure word of prophecy: whereunto ye do well that ye take heed, as unto a light that shineth in a dark place, until the dawn, and the day star arise in your hearts. Knowing this first, that no prophecy of the scripture is any private interpretation. For the prophecy came not in old time by the will of man: but holy men of God spake as they were moved by the Holy Ghost."*[58]

4. Pastor _____

A minister or priest serving a local church or parish.[59]

5. Teacher/Preacher _____

A person whose occupation is to give formal instruction in a school.[60] A related word to the teacher is a preacher. A preacher is a person specially trained and authorized to conduct religious services in a Christian church.[61] So, if you fall into the office of the teacher it would be relevant to notice that you are also a pastor.

The Apostle Paul wrote, *"And he gave some, apostles; and some prophets; and some, evangelists; and some, pastors and teachers; For the perfecting of the saints, for the work of the ministry, for the edifying of the body of Christ: Till we all come in the unity of the faith, and of the knowledge of the Son of God, unto a perfect man, unto the measure of the stature of the fullness of Christ: That we henceforth be no more children, tossed to and fro, and carried about with every wind of doctrine by the sleight of men, and cunning craftiness, whereby they lie in wait to deceive; But speaking the truth in love, may grow up into him in all things, which is the head, even Christ."*[62]

If you are unsure of the calling that God has placed upon your life, first pray to God asking for him to direct your path. Take one step at a time, there may be several offices that you have been called by God to walk in just study one office at a time gaining wisdom and understanding from God. Second, talk with your Pastor about this. Your Pastor is there for you and will help guide you in the right direction. Once you know your position in *the body of Christ,* continue to pursue God's heart and follow him in the position that he has placed upon your life.

What does the number 4 represent?

Jesus said, *"Say not ye, There are four months, and then cometh harvest? Behold, I say unto you, Lift up your eyes, and look on the fields; for they are white already to harvest."*[63] *There are four facts to point out here that Jesus states the harvest is already ready:*

1. The opportunity for the harvest for the kingdom of Heaven. Do you see the people in this world that need the love of Jesus? Of course you do. There are people that I have shared

the word of God with and they will not believe in God, or that Jesus is the Son of God. People who have responded to me in this way are walking in their flesh, they are *frozen* serving Satan, Jesus said to the Pharisees, *"Ye are they which justify yourselves before men; but God knoweth your hearts: for that which is highly esteemed among men is an abomination in the sight of God. The law and the prophets were until John: since that time the kingdom of God is preached, and every man presseth into it. And it is easier for heaven and earth to pass, than one tittle of the law to fail. Whosoever putteth away his wife, and marrieth another, committeth adultery: and whosoever marrieth her that is put away from her husband committeth adultery."*[64] You see the man that will not follow God's ways thinks that he is in control of his life, and therefore will continue to walk in his *fleshly spirit* and this man will die in his *fleshly spirit* over and over again in Hell as Satan torments his *fleshly spirit* for eternity. Jesus is in control of every life, one day everyone will face Jesus on their day of judgment and Jesus will determine where they will spend eternity, Heaven or Hell. Jesus said, *"For the Father judgeth no man, but hath committed all judgment unto the Son. That all men should honour the Son, even as they honour the Father. He that honoureth not the Son honoureth not the Father which hath sent him. Verily, verily, I say unto you, He that heareth my word, and believeth on him that sent me, hath everlasting life, and shall not come into condemnation: but is passed from death into life."*[65] I am not ashamed that Jesus is the Lord of my life. Jesus told us, *"For whosoever shall be ashamed of me and of my words, of him shall the Son of man be ashamed, when he shall come in his own glory and in his Father's, and of the holy angels."*[66] In your daily routine you will meet people, share the opportunity of knowing who Jesus is. Plain and simple Jesus is love. You could say, smile Jesus loves you that would spark up a conversation. Or, do you know Jesus loves you? If they say yes, say great I'm so happy you are my brother or sister in Jesus Christ, if they say no, or look dazed or confused, invite them to church with you. When you begin to walk in faith trusting in God's plan of salvation for everyone the domino effect will begin and not just the ninety nine sheep will be saved, the one that was lost will be saved, and all of Heaven will rejoice![67] All you need to do is plant the seed of *faith* for without the seed being planted by *faith it is impossible to please God.* Now faith is the substance of things hoped for, the evidence of things not seen.[68] But without faith it is impossible to please him: for he that cometh to God must believe that he is, and that he is a rewarder of them that diligently seek him.[69]

2. The workers for the harvest! Jesus is the Apostle, Prophet, Evangelist, Pastor & Teacher! Who has God called you to be?

"And he that reapeth receiveth wages, and gathereth fruit unto life eternal: that both that soweth and he that reapeth may rejoice together. And herein is that saying true, One soweth, and another reapeth."[70]

Jesus told us that we would do greater works than he, but in order for us to do these greater works for his kingdom we need to know who we are, then we need to follow through and step into the works that he has called us to.

3. The commitment to the harvest! *"I sent you to reap that whereon ye bestowed no labour, other men labored, and ye are entered into their labours."*[71] Be committed to the *harvest of souls, no one* should go to hell; Jesus Christ gave his life willingly, so that all of our sins would be forgiven. *We need to be the change that Jesus Christ says we can be!!!*

4. The obedience to the vision of Christ brings out the final truth ~*the joy of the harvest!* The definition of obedience is

submissive to the restraint or command of authority.[72] Jesus speaks of the workers' wages gathering fruit for *eternal life,* *"That both he who sows and he who reaps may rejoice together unto life eternal."*[73] When we are obedient, submitting our lives to the authority of God by choosing his will his vision we will receive eternal life in Heaven, Selah! Jesus said, *"Verily, verily, I say unto you, the Son can do nothing of himself, but what he seeth the Father do: for what things soever he doeth, these also doeth the Son likewise. For the Father loveth the Son, and sheweth him all things that himself doeth: and will shew him greater works than these, the ye may marvel."*[74]

Why is the frozen meat placed on the prayer shawl?

And the Lord spake unto Moses, saying, *"Speak unto the children of Israel, and bid them that they make them fringes in the borders a ribband of blue: And it shall be unto you for a fringe, that ye may look upon it, and remember all the commandments of the Lord, and do them; and that ye seek not after your own heart and your own eyes, after which ye use to go a whoring, That ye remember, and do all my commandments, and be holy unto your God. I am the Lord your God, which brought you out of the land of Egypt, to be your God: I am the Lord your God."*[75]

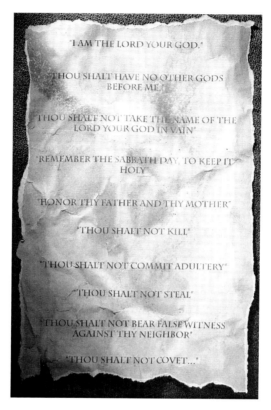

Why is the frozen meat out in the sun?

You can see the *sun* represents Jesus shining on all of the people in the Earth. Now when Jesus was risen early the first day of the week, he appeared first to Mary Magdalene, out of whom he had cast seven devils. And she went and told them that had been with him, as they mourned and wept. And they, when they had heard that he was alive, and had been seen of her, believed not. After that he appeared in another form unto two of them, as they walked, and went into the country. And they went and told it unto the residue: neither believed they them. Afterward he appeared unto the eleven as they sat at meat, and upbraided them with their unbelief and hardness of heart because they believed not them which had seen him after he was risen. And he said unto them, *"Go ye into all the world, and preach the gospel to every creature. He that believeth and is baptized shall be saved; but he that believeth not shall be damned. And these signs shall follow them that believe; In my name shall they cast out devils; they shall speak with new tongues; They shall take up serpents; and if they drink any deadly thing, it shall not hurt them they shall lay hands on the sick, and they shall recover."* So then after the Lord had spoken unto them, he was received up into heaven, and sat on the right hand of God. And they went forth, and preached everywhere, the Lord working with them, and confirming the word with signs following. Amen.[76]

"The mirror of my soul reflects the image of my Father, for all to see the light of Jesus shining from me, glory to God in the highest!"

The sun represents the light of Jesus that lives within his children! *"That ye may be the children of your Father which is in heaven: for he maketh his sun to rise on the evil and on the good, and sendeth rain on the just and on the unjust."*[77]

Jesus said, *"I am the light of the world; he that followeth me shall not walk in darkness, but shall have the light of life."*[78]

The white lion is a symbol of who we are walking in the purity of God's love; this is how God see's us. God has given us all authority it's time, for the bride to arise for the spirit of the Lord is in the bride! Arise and shine for your light has come, brothers and sisters![79]

"THE PROPHETIC SONG OF THE LORD"

"The Prophetic Song of the Lord" was released by the Lord to me on June 22, 2009 while in worship at home. As the Lord released this song over me, I was using my tape recorder and was able to record the entire prophecy. This prophecy from the Lord is about 10 minutes, and is typed out exactly the way it was released that day. During this word from the Lord, I could hear the Lord's voice and the sounds of his angels. As soon as the last word was given to me, a raven flew by and made an echoing croak filling the air. Ravens are considered ministers of God's justice and provision. Let's look at what happened to Elijah, And the word of the Lord came unto him, saying, *"Get thee hence, and turn thee eastward, and hide thyself by the brook Cherith, that is before Jordan. And is shall be, that thou shall drink of the brook; and I have commanded the raven to feed thee there."*[80] So he went and did according unto the word of the Lord: for he went and dwelt by the brook Cherith, that is before Jordan. And the ravens brought him bread and flesh in the morning, and bread and flesh in the morning, and bread and flesh in the evening; and he drank of the brook.

This "Prophetic Song of the Lord" is a confirmation of the word of God spoken throughout the bible by God and through God's Apostle, Prophets, Evangelists, Pastors and Teachers. As a disciple of Christ we are told, *"Study to shew thyself approved unto God, rightly dividing the word of truth."*[81] The Lord told me to write down where you can find this truth in his word enclosed in the different books of the Bible which is God's word for his children. Take comfort knowing God loves you bigger than you can even imagine! As you are breathing these words into your spirit expect a mighty move of God in your life, moving you into a deeper understanding of who God is and just how much he really loves you.

"THE SPIRIT OF THE LORD IS IN THE BRIDE"
(JOHN 3:8)

My Spirit's in the Bride (John 3:8)
My Spirit's in the Bride
You will arise (Mathew 25:6)
For I am coming soon (John 14:3)
Get ready for your King of Kings (Luke 3:4)
For he is coming soon (John 14:3)
Riding on a white horse (Revelation 3:4)
There is victory for you (1 John 5:4)

The Spirit of the Lord is in the Bride (John 3:8)
The Spirit of the Lord is in the Bride

For he is coming soon, to awaken' his Bride (Revelation 22:12)
Rise up ye saints (Isaiah 60:1)
Seek your King, diligently (Hebrew 11:6)
For Lord you will ride (Revelation 19:11)
Lord Christ you will ride
Prepare the way, for your King (Isaiah 40:3)
For there is victory, on the wings of love (1 John 5:4)
He is ready, to claim his Bride (John 14:3)

The Spirit of the Lord (2 Corinthians 3:17)
The Spirit of the Lord
The Spirit of the Lord
The Spirit of the Lord (ooh, ooh, ooh)
My people shall not suffer, they can bear no more (Mathew 24:22)
My heart is breaking for them, you're coming home (John 14:27)
My peace is with you child (John 15:26)
My peace is with you child
Hear this day from the Lord
The Spirit of the Lord is here, he is here with you (ooh, ooh)
The Spirit of the Lord is in the Bride
The Spirit of the Lord is in the Bride
The Spirit of the Lord (ooh, ooh, ooh)

Get ready for your King, the lion is ready to roar (Revelation 18:23)
Ready to claim his Bride
I am bringing her back to Heaven to live with me, by my side,
    eternally (John 14:3)
God's Spirit's in the Bride, God's Spirits in the Bride (Acts 2:1-4)
His Spirit is here (John 16:7-15)

The Lord says I'm coming soon (Revelation 22:12)
I am healing every wound for eternity (Revelation 22:2)
Do not be dismayed (Joshua 1:9)

For my word is true (Revelation 21:5)
For I am coming back for you (John 12:3)
I am coming back for you
I am coming back for you
Mighty warrior, you are a warrior in Christ (2 Timothy 2:3-4)
You will do greater works (John 14:12)
You will do many things (Ephesians 4:11)
You are ready to step into your calling, says the Lord (1
    Corinthians 12:28)
I will shield everyone, put on the armor of the Lord (Genesis 15:1)
The full armor of God (Ephesians 6:10-18)
My protection is nigh (Leviticus 10:3)
I am always with you my child (Mathew 28:20)
You have nothing to fear (Isaiah 41:10)
For I am hear with you (John 8:42)
You shall feel my presence (Psalm 114:7)
And you shall see me too, for the pure in heart will see the Lord
    (Mathew 5:8)
I said, the pure in heart shall see the Lord
My word is true, I died for you that day (Luke 23:46)
I died for you one day
And I rested in the arms of my Father, child (ooh, ooh, ooh)
    (Luke 23:46)
The dead in Christ will arise (1 Thessalonians 4:16, John 5:28-29)
The dead in Christ will arise
I am sending the witnesses (Revelation 11:3-6)
To oversee this plan
For they shall surely be with you, with you

I am ministering the "Song of the Lord" over a daughter of God. As I heard what God told me to sing over her, you can clearly see that she is receiving what God has for her. God's love permeated the atmosphere and the glory of the Lord was manifested. Jesus saith unto them, *"My meat is to do the will of him that sent me, and to finish his."*[82]

Walking in the obedience of God by reaching out for those who are in need of his love, releases God's love for his children through his children, directly from God. The love that God has for us takes away the pain and replaces that pain with love from God. Therefore, when we walk in that love that God bestows upon us, God delivers his love through us and his perfect love is then released within the body of Christ bringing healing and restoration throughout the body of Christ.

MY BRIDE DRESS IN HEAVEN
(DREAM TOOK PLACE MAY 5, 2009)

The Lord showed me a white silk bride dress and he placed a heart shaped gem that was gold in color at first in the center of the dress, then the gem turned deep purple. Then the Lord said, *"You have desired the gift of my healing love for my people and I am bestowing this gift upon you."* Then, he showed me the entire gown and at the bottom of the gown there were gems of all different colors that went completely around the dress in many rows that peaked up and down like mountains and were placed diligently.

See if you can discern this dream before looking at my interpretation!

What does the white silk gown represent?

_____

_____

_____

_____

What do the jewels represent on the dress?

_____

_____

_____

_____

Why do you believe that the jewels are placed in peaks like mountains?

_____

_____

_____

_____

Why do you believe that the Lord showed me a heart shaped gold gem then it turned a deep purple?

_____

_____

_____

_____

"You have desired the gift of my healing love for my people and I am bestowing this gift upon you." Why did God say this to me in this dream?

_____

_____

_____

_____

REVELATION OF BREAKING DOWN THE DREAM: "MY BRIDE DRESS IN HEAVEN"

Let's begin to breakdown this dream:

What does the white silk gown represent?

The silk gown is found in the *Proverbs 31 Woman*; *"She maketh herself coverings of tapestry; her clothing is silk and purple."*[83] The color white means *pure, "And to her was granted that she should be arrayed in fine linen, clean and white; for the fine linen is the righteousness of saints."*[84]

What do the jewels represent on the dress?

"I will greatly rejoice in the Lord, my soul shall be joyful in my God; for he hath clothed me with the garments of salvation, he hath covered me with the robe of righteousness, as a bridegroom decketh himself with ornaments, and as a bride adorneth herself with her jewels."[85]

Why do you believe that the jewels are placed in peaks like mountains?

When I saw the jewels placed in peaks like mountains right away the Lord told me that these were mountains that were in my life that I have overcome! Jesus answered and said unto them, *"Verily I say unto you, If ye have faith, and doubt not, ye shall not only do this which is done to the fig tree, but also if ye shall say unto this mountain, Be thou removed, and be thou cast into the sea; it shall be done. And all things, whatsoever ye shall ask in prayer, believing, ye shall receive."*[86] Wow!!! What a great promise from God! I have said this believing by faith over different circumstances that have risen in my life, and I have seen these mountains removed.

Why do you believe that the Lord showed me a heart shaped gold gem then it turned deep purple?

The heart shaped gem was gold first meaning Gods glory shining from within me. God knew that my desire is to receive the gift of *healing* from him, so God tells us in his holy word that he will give us the desires of our heart! King David tells us, *"Trust in the Lord, and do good; so shalt thou dwell in the land, and verily thou shalt be fed. Delight thyself also in the Lord: trust also in him; and he shall bring it to pass. And he shall bring forth thy righteousness as the light, and thy judgement as the noonday. Rest in the Lord, and wait patiently for him: fret not thyself because of him who prospereth in his way, because of the man who bringeth wicked devices to pass."* [87] Now what does the purple stone represent? The color purple signifies royalty, Then came Jesus forth, wearing the crown of thorns, and the purple robe.[88] We also see in God's word the *Proverbs 31 Woman, "She maketh herself coverings of tapestry; her clothing is silk and purple.*[89] In seeing the revelation of receiving this gift from God, first we see the glory of God shining from within my heart and then we see the gift of *healing* being released. Once we are born again receiving the baptism of the *Holy Spirit* we then in turn believe and trust on the word of God studying to understand who God is in our lives. Waiting patiently for God to release the revelation of who he is to us, be still and know that all will be given to you in God's timing.

"You have desired the gift of my healing love for my people and I am bestowing this gift upon you." Why did God say this to me in this dream?

God knows the desires of our hearts and when we ask praying to God, then we believe God for what we have asked him for God will do it, plain and simple. Jesus says, *"And all things, whatsoever ye shall ask in prayer, believing, ye shall receive."*[90]

God's character is that of *integrity*, the definition of *integrity* is faithfulness to high moral standards.[91] So when God tells us to ask and we shall receive he has *integrity*!!! *"Ask, and it shall be given you; seek, and ye shall find; knock, and it shall be opened unto*

you: For every one that asketh receiveth; and he that seeketh findeth; and to him that knocketh it shall be opened."[92] God also says to us you have not because you ask not. The Apostle John writes; "*These things have I written unto you that believe on the name of the Son of God; that ye may know that ye have eternal life, and that ye may believe on the name of the Son of God. And this is the confidence that we in him, that, if we ask any thing according to his will, he heareth us: And if we know that he hear us, whatsoever we ask, we know that we have the petitions that we desired of him.*"[93] Wow!!! *Absolute knowledge,* as we define *absolute* we see it means free from imperfection: free from control, restriction or qualification![94] As God speaks with us confirming in our lives we are walking out God's will for his absolute will for us. The Apostle Paul writes, "*Now then we are ambassadors for Christ, as though God did beseech you by us: we pray you in Christ's stead, be ye reconciled to God.*"[95] Let's break this down, since *ambassadors* are really citizens of another country, *the kingdom of heaven* they must do or not do certain things. An *ambassador* is a person sent on a mission to represent another.[96] Ambassadors are extraordinary and plenipotentiary. As we define extraordinary we see that we are notably unusual or exceptional.[97] As we define plenipotentiary we are a diplomatic agent having full authority![98] *We will walk in all authority on this earth as ambassadors for the kingdom of heaven, for God has given us all authority!*

In conclusion; God showed me my bride dress in Heaven, I need to also see that I am wearing this dress right now, knowing with the absolute knowledge God confirmed this to me through this dream so I would take comfort in knowing the position I need to take. We step into the positions that God has called us to walk in on this earth. This life is but a vapor, but the *kingdom of heaven is eternal* and *my spirit* will live forever in the kingdom of heaven with God!

VISION OF CHALLAH BREAD FILLED WITH MOZZARELLA CHEESE

(Vision took place March 2, 2011)

Our Father which art in heaven, Hallowed be thy Name.
Thy Kingdom come. Thy will be done, as in heaven so in
earth, Give us this day our daily bread. And forgive us our
sins; for we also forgive every one that is indebted to us. And
lead us not into temptation; but deliver us from evil.[99]

The Lord showed me a vision of a loaf of Challah Bread with
sesame seeds sprinkled on top. Then he showed me that the inside
of the bread was filled with shredded mozzarella cheese. I asked
the Lord, "Okay how do I get the cheese in the middle of the

bread?" Well, I was half asleep still and then he showed me divide the dough in two sprinkle the cheese in the middle and form the dough. Okay sounds simple Lord, now what does it mean!!! I have to laugh with the Lord because he gives me visions on a constant basis and I am always seeking him to know what they mean. So I now I have asked the Lord, "Can I have more of you Lord?" Well, the Lord always answers our prayers, if we seek the Lord we will find him and then he can direct our paths. Why you ask did the Lord show me a vision of this, here is my journey ready, set, go!!!

bread?" Well, I was half asleep still and then he showed me divide the dough in two sprinkle the cheese in the middle and form the dough. Okay sounds simple Lord, now what does it mean!!! I have to laugh with the Lord because he gives me visions on a constant basis and I am always seeking him to know what they mean. So I now I have asked the Lord, "Can I have more of you Lord?" Well, the Lord always answers our prayers, if we seek the Lord we will find him and then he can direct our paths. Why you ask did the Lord show me a vision of this, here is my journey ready, set, go!!!

Challah or hallah is traditional Jewish bread eaten on Shabbat and Jewish holidays (except Passover, when leavened bread is not allowed). Lord why Challah Bread and not Carmelized Onion Focaccia? The Lord says, the two are very different and I will show you a picture of what I am trying to get through to you that you will understand. Okay so it is already formed and cooked and ready to eat! I can understand that Lord now let's eat. The Lord laughs at me not just yet, Sherry for you are not finished interpreting this vision from me. Okay Lord then what do we look at next? List the ingredients used when you make this bread and then discern what they mean:

Water Baptism ("Water Baptism" is to be "Born Again" to be cleansed for the remission of sins once you receive the water baptism you receive the Holy Spirit): *"Verily, verily, I say unto thee, Except a man be born of water and of the Spirit, he cannot enter into the kingdom of God. That which is born of the flesh is flesh; and that which is born of the Spirit is spirit. Marvel not that I said unto thee, Ye must be born again. The wind bloweth where it listeth, and thou hearest the sound thereof, but canst not tell whence it cometh, and whither it goeth: so is every one that is born of the Spirit."*[100]

Oil (the Holy Spirit): *"I have found David my servant; with my holy oil have I anointed him."*[101]

Whole Egg (Ask & you will receive): *"If a son shall ask bread of any of you that is a father, will he give him a stone? Or if he ask a fish, will he for a fish give him a serpent? Or if he shall ask an egg, will he offer him a scorpion? If ye then, being evil, know how to give good gifts unto your children: how much more shall your heavenly Father give the Holy Spirit to them that ask him?"*[102]

Butter (Revelation of the Word of God): *"Butter and honey shall he eat, that he may know to refuse the evil and chose the good."*[103]

Milk (New Christians need the milk first): *"As newborn babes, desire the sincere milk of the word, that ye may grow thereby."*[104]

Bread flour ("The Wheat" are the Righteous of God): *"Let both grow together until the harvest I will say to the reapers, Gather ye together first the tares, and bind them in bundles to burn them: but gather the wheat into my barn."*[105]

Mozzarella Cheese (Meat): Jesus saith unto them, *"My meat is to do the will of him that sent me, and to finish his work."*[106] Jesus is stating here that his food or nourishment comes from doing the will God and to finish his work.

Salt: (To keep the covenant of God or to break his covenant): *"And if thine eye offend thee, pluck it out: it is better for thee to enter into the kingdom of God with one eye, than having two eyes to be cast into hell fire: Where their worm dieth not, and the fire is not quenched. For every one shall be salted with fire, and every sacrifice shall be salted with salt. Salt is good: but if the salt have lost his saltness, wherewith will ye season it? Have salt in yourselves, and have peace one with another."*[107]

Sugar (Fruit of the Spirit): *"But the fruit of the Spirit is love, joy, peace, longsuffering, gentleness, goodness, faith, meekness, temperance: against such there is no law. And they that are Christ's have crucified the flesh with the affections and lusts. If we live in the Spirit, let us also walk in the Spirit. Let us not be desirous of vain glory, provoking one another, envying one another."*[108]

Sesame Seeds (Manna): Now to Abraham and his seed were the promises made. He saith not, *"And to seeds, as of many; but as of one, And to thy seed which is Christ."*[109] The seeds represent manna which God gave to the Israelites while they wandered in the desert.

Yeast or Leaven (Being Born Again/Repentance): Another parable spake he unto them; *"The Kingdom of Heaven is like unto leaven, which a woman took, and hid in three measures of meal, till the whole was leavened."* All these things spake Jesus unto the multitude in parables: and without a parable spake he not unto them: *"That it might be fulfilled which was spoken by the prophet, saying, I will open my mouth in parables; I will utter things which have been kept secret from the foundation of the world."*[110] The Kingdom spreads like yeast!

Rest (the dough needs to rest and as the dough rests it rises to perfection): *"But they that wait upon the Lord shall renew their strength; they shall mount up with wings as eagles; they shall run, and not be weary; and they shall walk, and not faint."*[111] As you are praying and worshipping the Lord he is renewing your strength you will run in the call that the Lord has placed upon your life. Know that God is always with you he will never leave you or forsake you. Jesus was fasting in the desert when Satan came to him saying to turn the stones into bread. Satan was trying to get Jesus to walk in his flesh instead of staying focused on the word of God. Jesus told Satan that man can't live by bread alone that man must live by every word that comes out of the mouth of God. For the words of God are life to our spirit.

Fire/Oven to cook (the Holy Spirit): *"And there appeared unto them cloven tongues like as of fire, and it sat upon each of them. And they were all filled with the Holy Ghost, and began to speak with other tongues, as the Spirit gave them utterance."*[112]

Let's not forget that we must mold the dough with our hands into the shape of a loaf of bread. God has made us in his image, his big hands are the potter and we are the clay. After you mold the bread you take a knife and cut into the dough so when the dough rises it will not lose its shape. Much like how God does with us consider this metaphor, the knife used to cut into the dough is the word of God and the dough is our flesh. For the word of God is quick, and powerful, and sharper than any two-edged sword, piercing even to the dividing asunder of soul and spirit, and of the joints and marrow, and is a discerner of the thoughts and intents of the heart.[113] Then, you brush the dough with the egg and water mixture all over the dough to give the bread a beautiful golden luster. Let's assimilate this with how God deals with us, when we cast all of our burdens on God we see that his yoke is easy and his burden is light. When we receive the baptism of the Holy Spirit we are *born again,* no longer walking in *the flesh* now we are walking in *the spirit.* Jesus answered, *"Verily, verily, I say unto thee, Except a man be born of water and of the Spirit, he cannot enter into the kingdom of God. That which is born of the flesh is flesh; and that which is born of the Spirit is spirit. Marvel not that I said unto thee, Ye must be born again. The wind bloweth where it listeth, and thou hearest the sound thereof, but canst not tell whence it cometh, and whither it goeth: so is every one that is born of the Spirit."*[114] We sprinkle the sesame seeds on the top of the dough; this represents the manna that God gave to the Israelites while they wandered in the desert. God is our provider we need to trust in him knowing that his ways are higher than ours. Next we let the dough rest and as the dough rests it rises to perfection. Much like when we pray and worship God resting in his *perfect love,* God is renewing our strength imparting a deeper revelation of who he is to us, he is opening up his heart for us to receive a greater understanding of knowledge of who he is in our lives. Then we place the dough in the hot oven and bake it until it is no longer doughy on the inside or outside, and you see a golden luster on the outside of the bread. Our God is an all consuming fire and as we are learning God's laws our flesh is no longer soft and mushy following Satan, we are following God and our flesh is strong and able to withstand the fiery darts that Satan tries to send our way. Those darts bounce off of us. Imagine a soft dough the darts would stick into the dough but a baked dough has the armor of God on and can't be penetrated by those darts. We must know the word of God to be able to stand through the trials that this life we live in throws our way. Taking refuge in God, abiding in his presence with his wings of love wrapped around us he will never leave us or forsake us. God is love and as we walk in unity with God we will reflect his love. Now imagine the bread cooking in the oven, the sweet smell of fresh baked bread is a beautiful aroma. As you are breathing in the aroma of the bread baking you can just taste the bread melting in your mouth, your mouth begins to water anticipating the first bite of that delicious bread. When we feel hungry for a slice of bread, this is really our soul's desire for its spiritual essence. Food feeds body and spirit. I am spiritually nourished. Food is not about simply keeping me alive. It is about helping me live for the purpose for which I was created having a spiritual relationship with God my father.

Assimilate the Challah Bread to living your life as God's child, for he is your Father. When you are following God, diligently seeking him then you are an overcomer through Jesus Christ and you will enter the gates of Heaven along with those children that God has placed upon your path to teach Gods word and show them how much God loves them. Can you imagine the love of God, giving his only son Jesus Christ so that you could have a choice to spend eternity in Heaven with him? As you thank God throughout the day God is glorified. God rains down his tears from Heaven over you, for God created you in his image; he loves to spend time with you. Take time throughout your day to seek

God's will for you, he is always with you, just stop for a moment cry out to God and you will feel his presence encompassing you. Always praying, believing that you have received, and then thanking God for what you have asked God for. Always thank God for he is worthy of all your praise, worshipping God in spirit and truth knowing that he is your provider.

God said to me, *"Continue to pursue me diligently with all of your mind, soul, heart and physical strength. Taste and see that the Lord is good, for you can't make a loaf of Challah bread without these ingredients if you are missing one it will not be the same."*

THE PINK ANGEL FEATHER

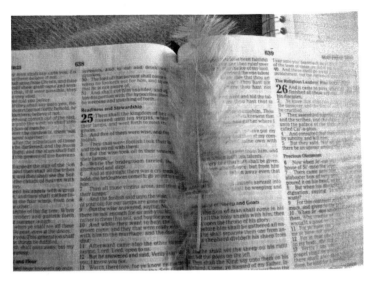

This is the *pink angel* feather that was placed in my right
shoe after a warning dream from God; the bone of this
feather is pink and the feathers radiate a *pink iridescence*

This *pink angel feather* was found in my right shoe that I wear
when I walk my dogs. My shoes are kept on a white metal shelf
inside my garage. I had put them away before going to bed the
night before this dream, on this shelf. When I went to put my
shoes on the next morning the feather was inside my right shoe,
meaning that God wanted me to see that the *pink angel* that I
had seen at the beginning of this warning dream was real, so that
I would share this warning with my friend. God's angel placed

her feather inside my shoe so that when I put my shoes on, I would feel the presence of God and then when I pulled my foot out, I would see the manifestation of God, knowing the angel was real and that God was directing me to share this warning with the friend that this dream was about. I did share the dream with my friend and he understood exactly what the dream meant. God will use his angels to relay his messages to us. Jesus was in the wilderness, and was tempted by Satan, God his Father sent his angels to minister to Jesus! *"And he was there in the wilderness 40 days, tempted of Satan; and was with the wild beasts; and the angels ministered unto him."*[115] Also see, *"And there appeared an angel unto him from heaven, strengthening him. And being in an agony he prayed more earnestly: and his sweat was as it were great drops of blood falling down to the ground."*[116] Angels are all around us, they are mentioned throughout the Old Testament and the New Testament! I have had many dreams and visions with angels in them. There is one angel in particular that I have seen several times in different dreams; he is my guardian angel. He is tall, with tan skin, long blonde hair to this shoulders; he wears a white linen button down shirt, and light blue denim jeans, no shoes, and I have never seen his wings. I've prayed to God about the angel not having shoes on, and he released this to me, *"The angels are praising, worshipping me and the ground that they walk on is holy ground there are no shoes worn,"* then God said this is what I told Moses, *"Draw not hither: put off thy shoes from thy feet, whereon thou standest is holy ground."*[117] Also, why doesn't he have wings? The bible speaks of angels without wings; they are a spirit being meaning they can go anywhere they want to, they do not need wings to get to where they are going. Another point to see is that there are angels mentioned in the bible that are female and male. Let's reference this scripture to see the female angels, *"Then lifted I up mine eyes, and looked and, behold, there came out two women, and the wind was in their wings; for they had wings like the wings of a stork: and they lifted up the ephah between the earth and the heaven."*[118] Let's reference this scripture to see the male angels, *"And there was war in heaven: Michael and his angels fought against the dragon; and the dragon fought and his angels. And prevailed not; neither was their place found any more in heaven. And the great dragon was cast out, that old serpent, called the devil, and Satan, which deceiveth the whole world; he was cast out into the earth, and his angels were cast out with him."*[119]

My guardian angel shows me what direction I am to take with God, he gives encouragement; he warns me of impending danger; and he shows me things that are to come for the church. In prayer with God, I asked God what is my guardian angel's name, and I heard God say his name is Mark! You know me, I have to look up now what Mark means; martial, warlike![120] Wow, God surely has me protected! Once I was following him as he led me into a room and he pulled up a chair in front of me, flipped the chair around, and sat in the chair with the back of the chair in front of him leaning in towards me, explaining to me a vision from God. What he showed me was an outline of the United States of America, and I could see all of the states rightly divided, and then within each state I could see flames of fire spreading till the flames ignited within every state and he even showed me who I was to minister with in doing this! So, Mark's assignment was to "coach" me in the skills that I will need to accomplish this. God's angels are ministers of flaming fire, see right here in the word of God, *"Who maketh his angels spirits; his ministers a flaming fire!"*[121] God's angels are ministers of flaming fire delivering God's message to his children, hallelujah let's praise the Lord for only he is holy and worthy of all of our praise he never leaves us he is always directing our path!

God will show you warnings about people that you know and when you pray for them and intercede God will intervene on your behalf because you are being obedient to what God is speaking with you. The effectual fervent prayer of a righteous man availeth much. God will show you dreams/visions that you will only share with certain people, not everyone needs to know every dream that God releases to you. As you walk with God in this area, he is watching you to see just how obedient that you will be releasing his wisdom in the way that he wants you to release it. The more you understand the way God uses symbols to speak with you, the better understanding you will have when God releases a dream or vision. When you release a word over someone from a dream/vision, always try to discern what you *see* interpreting the dream/vision into words that will be understood by the person listening to you. If you say, *"I see this huge red dragon grabbing you by the back of your neck"* people would look you funny, become afraid of you and think that you are crazy, and not understand what you are interpreting from God. Instead you would say, *"Satan is holding you back from what God has for you."* To define the *red dragon*, *"And there appeared another wonder in heaven; and behold a great red dragon, having seven heads and ten horns, and seven crowns upon his heads. And his tail drew the third part of the stars of heaven, and did cast them to the earth: and the dragon stood before the woman which was ready to be delivered, for to devour her child as soon as it was born."*[122] To define what the *red dragon* is doing we look at what God says about *stiff necked* people, And the Lord said unto Moses, *"Go, get thee down; for thy people, which thou broughtest out of the land of Egypt, have corrupted themselves: They have turned aside quickly out of the way which I commanded them: they have made them a molten calf, and have worshipped it, and have sacrificed thereunto,"* and said, *"These be thy gods, O Israel, which have brought thee up out of the land of Egypt. And the Lord said unto Moses, I have seen this people, and, behold, it is a stiffnecked people."*[123] After God has revealed many dream/visions to you and you have diligently taken the time to search out God's heart when you see a dream/vision you will be able to quickly reference what God is saying. If you do not take God seriously when he starts to release dreams/ visions over you, then God will not continue to show you more. I am not saying that you will need to speak out the scripture in detail after the discernment, however, that would be awesome if you could I am only saying that once you know how God speaks with you through situations about other people and you know God's word, you will be able to prophesy with more accuracy when you *see* a vision to discern. God will tell you what to say when you step out in *faith* knowing that he is always with you.

ANGELS IN THE NICU

My son Isaac was born on April 24, 2010. He was diagnosed with two holes in his heart, and he was having a very difficult time breathing due to this condition. A specialist was sent in to do an ultrasound of his heart. The doctor told me that he had a very large hole that would need surgery. You see, I had a similar experience when my daughter Christina was born on April 29, 2004. She was born with a large hole in her heart; the doctor told me that her heart sounded like a washing machine. The doctor told us that when she was 6 weeks of age they would need to do open heart surgery to repair her heart. My husband and I prayed to God her healing asking him to heal her. We took her to her 6 week appointment with the pediatric cardiologist and as he was doing a very extensive ultrasound he said this to us, "Your daughter is completely healed, I see no evidence of a hole any longer, she will not need surgery and her heart is strong." Praise the Lord! We all rejoiced knowing and thanking God for healing Christina. You see, there is something that is "very important" to know when you are praying to God for healing. "Know that you know, that you know that you know that God is our healer, and *never* let any vain imaginations or lie come in from Satan. So, when the doctor's told my husband and I about our son Isaac and his condition, I looked at my husband Steven and said, "*We*

have fought this giant before, I know exactly how to slay this one!"
So we began to pray to God, I said Lord, you healed Christina
from this same affliction and I declare right now in the name
of your son Jesus Christ that Isaac is healed!" While we were in
the hospital, I would walk to the NICU and hold Isaac praying
over him and singing over him, the nurses even sang over him
when I was sleeping! I knew that God had Isaac in his hands.
God made a promise to me before I even had Isaac, one morning
as I was praying I said to God, *"Lord I am in a dry season, I ask
that you would bless me and enlarge my territory, then I surely would
know that your hand is with me."* Then God spoke he declared in
a loud voice of might, *"You will have a son and his name will be
called, Isaac!"* Well, I burst out laughing I said really Lord, I am
41 years old, and I am not so sure about the name Isaac Conrad,
that doesn't really flow together. I told my husband and children
and they all laughed as well. God loves to confirm what he has
spoken with me and after that happened, I would be driving and
see a sign with the name Isaac. Or I would meet someone with
the name Isaac. I looked up what the name Isaac means, it means
he will laugh.[124]

Back to the hospital, the doctor's said that they were going
to take him off of the oxygen and heart monitor and see how he
did because they were starting to see Isaac's health improving. So,
they brought Isaac to my room and I was able to hold him in my
arms without being hooked up to any machines. In that moment
with the doctor and nurse on *standby* just in case he started to
code, I look at Isaac remembering what God's promise was to me
for Isaac. Then I looked up at the clock in front of me and knew
at that moment that God had kept his word. After that moment
Isaac was able to stay in my room, they took all of the tubes
and did another ultrasound and the holes were closed! Praise the
Lord! I remember this one doctor who came into my room for
a brief moment and said to me, "I have been watching your son,

and in all of my years of practice, I have never seen a miracle such as this, God has surely blessed you!" I smiled at him with tears rolling down my face and said, "Yes, God has healed him!" I have included a picture from that time and you will see bright balls of light that represent God's ministering flames of fire at work, God's angels. The word of God tells us this, *"Every good gift and every perfect gift is from above, and cometh down from the Father of lights, with whom is no variableness, neither shadow of turning."*[125] I thank you God for healing Christina and Isaac they are such wonderful blessings in my life from you God!

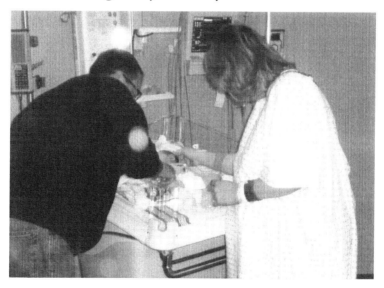

FOR HE SHALL GIVE HIS ANGELS CHARGE OVER THEE; TO KEEP THEE IN ALL THY WAYS.[126]

On the eve of April 8, 2011, I took my one year old son Isaac into my bedroom to sing over him before he fell asleep. As I was singing to him, light began to fill the room that was only lit by a night light. To my right I saw large white wings with feathers, and then more angels came into my room and the angels began to encompass us. As I watched and sang, I could see the detail of their wings, they sparkled with such beauty; they continued circling around Isaac and I. Then, presence of God filled my room and the love that I felt in that moment, drew me back to that time when Jesus appeared to me at the door of my home just twelve years earlier in my life. The love of Jesus is like no other love that I can compare to describe just how much he loves us. As his presence filled my room my son and I were enveloped in the love of God. Then I began to sing a new song. God gave me a new song in that moment it is called "Angels," with the words and the melody. How beautiful to hear the angels sing over us, such peace, I heard female and male voices echoing this song. Declaring God's protection over us; *"For he shall give his angels charge over thee; to keep thee in all thy ways."*[127] I'm not quite sure just how long that moment lasted, my prayer would be God let this moment last for an eternity. I just didn't want to move. The love of my Father was just so great, his arms are so strong, his words penetrate to the core of my heart, his wisdom reveals who I am in him, and his love is like a two-edged sword that cuts through any fear that the enemy will try to invade your life with yet covers every sings the enemy tries to hinder your life with. *The perfect love* of God casts out all fear and brings forth this revelation.[128] Nothing is too great that God's love can't overcome! So, God will reveal any hidden areas of your life that Satan will try to hide from you, so you will not stay in that sin as to not be able to achieve the perfect will for your life that God has for you and other's as well. God comes in and shows us his love, revealing what it is that we are holding back, and shines his love on that obstacle/sin taking away all of it and restoring our hearts and souls. As you listen to the song, *Angels* you will feel the presence of God's perfect love and the presence of his angels encompassing you.

TAKEN FROM HELL'S FIRE, AND PLACED IN FRONT OF THE GATES OF HEAVEN

God's word says that when we teach our children about him that our children will never depart from him.[129] My children have been taught God's word, and have a relationship with God. When you know God, he will reveal the secrets of his heart to you.[130] I would like to share two dreams with you that my ten year old son Andrew had recently. I feel that they are imperative to share with you. Why? God's timing is always perfect, why would God impart this revelation of Hell and Heaven to my son Andrew during this time? I asked my son Andrew, why do you think that God showed you Hell? Andrew replied, "God showed me Hell mom because he wanted me to see where you would have spent eternity if you didn't forgive Jesus when he visited with you after you lost your babies." Well, that reply pierced my heart, quickening the Holy Spirit within me that Andrew knew the truth and that he has a relationship with God and that was why God took Andrew to Heaven as well. God revealed my mansion, my library and the grand room, along with many other aspects of Heaven. You see God wanted Andrew to know that he forgave me and that I would spend eternity in Heaven with him. God also revealed to Andrew that I was this famous author in Heaven. I will tell you this friend; I am very humbled to have this opportunity to share with you my experiences with God. It is truly my heart as it is the heart of God that you will receive an impartation that will open your eyes and ears to a deeper revelation of who God is. So, after Andrew revealed his dreams to me, I heard God speak with me telling me to share Andrew's dreams with you. God told me to interview Andrew and that this type of ministry would open up a new door for other people to share their experiences. As I continue on this journey, the battle has been challenging, there have been times that I have felt like I am at the top of a large mountain and fiery darts are being plummeted towards me, but I laugh in the face of the enemy knowing that God shields me from those fiery darts knowing that no weapon formed against me will ever prosper, knowing that I will dig my heels in the ground and stand firm on the word of God not being swayed by any attack that the enemy tries to throw my way. For the battle belongs to the Lord, and I lay all of my cares at the feet of Jesus, for his yoke is easy and his burden is light, how do I know this? Easy, I know the word of God; I have a relationship with God that is like no other. I place God first and foremost in my life, the experiences that you are about to read about are true in every way. There is one important fact that I would like to point out here in reference to Andrew's experience in Hell. Andrew saw Satan in his true form, which I have seen before in a vision during prayer once, I believe that I saw Satan in this form so I could relate to how Andrew felt and I could pray over him. Satan is very intimidating to look at, and you can just feel the hatred emanating from his spirit towards you. It is Satan's plan to kill, steal and destroy your spirit for eternity. You see your spirit lives on, and will live for eternity in Heaven or in Hell. God has given you a free will to choose where your "spirit" will spend eternity; your "spirit" is who you are. Walk in wisdom having the fear of the Lord by choosing Heaven with God where you will live in peace for eternity. No one should spend eternity in Hell, no one. Don't believe the lie of Satan when he tells you to wait another day and then you will give your life to God, for we are *not promised tomorrow!* At the beginning of this book I was taken from Hell's fire…and placed in front of the gates of Heaven by one act of repentance. Jesus said, *"I am not to blame, your children are safe inside the gates of heaven, now come and let me in. Behold, I come to save you for I am not to blame, your children are safe in heaven one day you three shall meet."* That one act of repentance on my part took away the pain of Hell from my spirit and replaced the pain with the love of Jesus Christ. Jesus not only saved me that day, Jesus saved my children and they are living right now for eternity inside the gates of Heaven with my family and friends that have moved forward to eternity in Heaven. We are promised eternity in Heaven when we accept Jesus Christ as our Lord and Saviour, God's word says, "For God so loved the world that he gave his only begotten son, that whosoever believeth in him should not perish but have everlasting life."[131] We also must be baptized with water to enter the kingdom of God. Jesus answered, "Verily, verily, I say unto thee, Except a man be born of water and of the Spirit, he cannot enter into the kingdom of God. That which is born of the flesh is flesh; and that which is born of the Spirit is spirit. Marvel not that I said unto thee, Ye must be born again.[132] We must receive the Holy Spirit through accepting Jesus Christ as our Lord and Saviour in our life, you see when we are first born in this "world" we are born with sin the bible makes this clear. As it is written, *"There is none righteous, no, not one."*[133] We are all sinners in need of mercy and forgiveness from God.[134] Not by works of righteousness which we have done, but according to his mercy he saved us, by the washing of regeneration, and renewing of the Holy Ghost; Which he shed on us abundantly through Jesus Christ our Saviour; That being justified by his grace, we should be made heirs according to the hope of eternal life. Because of our sin we deserve eternal punishment.[135] And these shall go away into everlasting punishment: but the righteous into life eternal. And how do you benefit if you gain the whole world but lose your own soul in the process? Is anything worth more than your soul?[136]

ANDREW'S DREAM: HELL'S FIRE (DECEMBER 17, 2012)

Andrew: I was at this lake, it was bubbling and boiling with fire, like lava I saw this man he did not smell really good, he smelled like fish, dead fish. He had this really bad grin, he went to shake my hand but I stepped away. He got really angry and he turned red and his legs were furry he had hooves and he had horns, that were like a ram. Satan was angry and the lake of fire started to shoot out big bursts of fire into the air because he was angry.

Mom: Andrew saw the lake of fire.[137] Andrew said that he smelled like dead fish this is because *fish* represent all of mankind.[138] The color red in this dream refers to hatred and anger.[139] Andrew said that his legs were furry and he had hooves and he had horns that were like a ram. I asked Andrew if he had two legs or four and he said two legs.[140] I am referring to the satyr in this scripture that is defined as a woodland deity in Greek mythology having certain characteristics of a horse or goat.[141] What did he look like before he turned into that creature?

Andrew: He looked like a man with black hair, and a black tee shirt, black pants and black shoes. And he was not wearing any socks.

Mom: Black represents sin and the fact that Andrew recalls that the man was not wearing any socks, is important as well.[142] To have no socks on would represent that he is not walking in the gospel of peace.[143] *Was he trying to grab your hand with his left hand or right hand?*

Andrew: It was his left hand.

Mom: The left hand refers to judgment; Satan was trying to pull you into Hell.[144]

Andrew: *What does the right hand mean?*

Mom: The right hand represents the position of authority that we have with God.[145]

Andrew: Then he got really mad. His eyebrows were not that big, but big. He was really mad; he grabbed me by my throat.

Mom: *Describe his appearance in detail.*

Andrew: He was really muscular with a lot of abs. He's really strong; he looked like a guy that would work out every day, and wouldn't stop, nonstop, not even to go to the bathroom.

Mom: Look at this description "he looked like a guy that would work out every day, and wouldn't even stop, nonstop."[146] Look at this: "not even to go to the bathroom" the devil doesn't go to the bathroom because he represents all sin.[147]

Andrew: And he grabbed me by the throat, threw me down into the lake, going down into the lake with me and when I hit the ground there were these demons. They didn't have any eyes and had this nose that was black kind of like on the cartoons.

Mom: *Did it look like a skull?* See this, "and he grabbed me by the throat" those who follow Satan's ways will one day owe their soul to Satan for eternity, Satan receives your soul for eternity to torture for it belongs to him.[148] God allowed Andrew to experience this so that he could warn the world about Satan and his demons in Hell. Demons are seen throughout the bible here is just one passage to reference (Mathew 18:34). Children are pure in heart and they will see the Lord.[149]

Andrew: Yeah, a skull nose, and then it had these teeth that were really big and very sharp with blood on them, not a lot just some to tell there was blood. There were four of them and their bodies were pure black, all you could see was the blood, the teeth and the breath was horrible. There were bones down there, it smelled like dead people. I saw two bulls. One was a regular bull, but with knife hands.

Mom: God says that there will be weeping and gnashing of teeth this is why Andrew saw their teeth with blood on them they are torturing those who are in Hell for eternity over and over again.[150] *Were his hands like one knife or like little knives coming out?*

Andrew: One hand had a little knife on it, and one had a big machete on it. Then the other bull had a stitched eye kind of like it was pulled out, and one regular eye. It had hooves to hit people with, and when you went to the gray door that was really hot you could hear all the people screaming, "Help me, help me!!!" when that happened I was just really scared and then I looked at God, he's like "Don't be afraid this is not where you are ending up to go."

Mom: Bulls represent fierce and relentless adversaries;[151] it is interesting to note that one of the bulls had a stitched eye that looked like it was pulled out of its socket eyes that do not see.[152] The color gray represents the gray area between right and wrong, the wrong door was chosen on Earth by the people that are being tormented behind this door, these people are rebellious chose to follow Satan and not God now they will be tormented for all eternity. [153]Andrew heard the people screaming out, "Help me, help me!!!" God's word tells us that if we do not abide in him that we will be thrown into the fire and will be burned.[154] God told Andrew, "Don't be afraid this is not where you are ending up to go." God is perfect love and the *love of God casts out all fear*![155] *God was there? You could see God?*

Andrew: I couldn't really see him, I looked up and it was like gold, and I listened to him, I couldn't see anything just gold. Like kind of like an opening of the clouds, but there weren't any clouds. Then the devil had a grin, he was just smiling and I was like what is he smiling about? Then the ground started shaking and then it flew open, then when I fell down there, there was this lake of fire; there was this huge frog with horns, kind of like the devils horns except the frog's horns stuck out. The devil got on top of the frog riding him, the frog tried to stab me with it but I moved out of the way. The devil was laughing and I was scared to death. God opened up an area where I could see his hands. They were really big. God has really good trimmed nails it smelled really good. The entire place smelled really good, because of God's presence.

Mom: Andrew saw gold with an opening of the clouds, we see in the God's word that represents Gods presence and guidance remember how God lead the Israelites with a pillar of a cloud during the day and a pillar of fire by night to give them light.[156] Andrew says that the devil had a grin, he was smiling trying to invoke fear into Andrew of what was going to happen next and then Andrew was startled when the ground started shaking and then it flew open and Andrew fell down there and there was another lake of fire, and then Andrew saw this huge frog that had horns that were sticking out, the devil got on top of the frog and the frog was trying to pierce Andrew with his horns as the devil was laughing because Andrew was scared to death. God's hands are large he made this entire world and God is in control of everything that happens his hands are big enough to hold everything in them. I believe that it is significant that Andrew saw God's nicely manicured finger nails, God loves cleanliness. *What would you say it smelled like?*

Andrew: It smelled like really good perfume and marshmallows. And he said, "Don't be afraid Andrew, you're not ending up here, and they can't hurt you. I'm protecting you with my angels." In that moment, I was really happy because I was like, you can't touch me, and then I was like you better get vacuuming and stuff because this place is filthy. God picked me up and placed me directly into the gates of Heaven.

Mom: God told Andrew, "Don't be afraid Andrew, you're not ending up here, and they can't hurt you. I'm protecting you with my angels."[157] You see God is our refuge and he will protect us because God loves us, remember when Moses and the Israelites were leaving Egypt which was the land of bondage, God wanted his children to rest in the Promised Land. However, when they were leaving the Pharaoh and his army came after them do you remember what God did at that moment, Moses trusted in God and held out his rod and God parted the Red Sea for Moses and the Israelites so that they could cross over to safety into the promised land which is heaven, once they made it across God closed the Red Sea on the Pharaoh and his army, the horse and the rider where cast into the sea.[158] God will never leave you or forsake you when you are trusting in him to guide your path you will spend eternity in Heaven with him. God used his left and right hands because only God can take you out of the pit of Hell's fire, only God has the authority to do this. God picked Andrew up with his big hands and safely placed him directly in front of the gates of Heaven where Andrew will spend eternity with him!

ANDREW'S DREAM: INSIDE THE GATES OF HEAVEN (DECEMBER 18, 2012)

Andrew: God placed me in front of the gates of Heaven, I went up to this gate, and it had all sorts of diamonds, and colors, and gems that you have never seen before but in Heaven each gem has a name that we have never heard before and it does not sound weird. The gate was pure gold. The gems were really different, and like pink with green and brown with gold, and when the gate opened, I saw my mom's mansion. It was pure gold, there was a sidewalk that was gold that curved leading to the door of my mom's mansion, and when you opened the door, it smelled really good, the gold wall, had blue gems, all across and diamonds.

Mom: Andrew says that the gate had all sorts of diamonds, and colors, and gems that you have never seen before but in heaven each gem has a name that we have never heard before and it does not sound weird.[159] *Did they look like sapphires or dark blue?*

Andrew: No they were turquoise. I thought your favorite color was pink mom?

Mom: I like pink; however, turquoise is my favorite color. God truly knows our heart he made us and only he truly knows our favorite things.[160] *The gold mansion sounds exquisite! Where they mixed in?*

Andrew: No, a row like this with diamonds and a row of turquoise gems. The gems were layered first one row, then another and every wall in your mansion looked like this. There was a staircase that led up to where your bedroom is. When you go into the bedroom it smelled like marshmallows and you have a bed, that had this one thing that made you very sleepy, and it was very soft which was silver. Your pillow was gold. The one that's on top of the little blanket is pure gold too! The silver one under it is really soft. You had this radio that would be on this counter and when you turn it on it would have these trumpets playing and you have these cds, and they'd be like the best cds you would want to listen to them nonstop. In your bedroom was your wedding picture of you and dad, and inside the wedding picture were your wedding rings. Then, you'd have this library; it was gold, kind of like the White House but better.

Mom: *What do you mean like the White House?*

Andrew: The ancient place, kind of like Abraham Lincoln had with columns and stuff except not Abraham Lincoln, and it had a door.

Mom: So now I am laughing…what Andrew is saying is that my library in Heaven is a great big building similar to the White House where the 16th President of the United States of America Abraham Lincoln once lived, however, not exactly like the White House my Gold Library in Heaven is much better. *Okay so it was a separate building from my house?*

Andrew: Yes, it was about 1,000 feet from where your house was. The streets were gold and very wide.

Mom: *This was my library?*

Andrew: Yes, your own library. The title of it was *Sherry's Novels.*

Mom: *Was that on the outside of my Gold Library?*

Andrew: Yes, it had this gold thing, and the words were white so you could see them. Then you'd open the door and it smelled really good. It smelled like perfume, not like that one that smelled bad. Then, my favorite thing that you had in there was the desk, and you'd have the computer with a scanning thing. Then you'd be able to write a book and no one could tell you that's wrong. Like you have to change this and that, unless you want to. Then there would be these books, and one of the book's title, was *The Arriving of the King.*

Mom: *It was a book that I wrote?*

Andrew: Yes.

Mom: *What was the color of the book Andrew?*

Andrew: The book was red and purple.

Mom: I am writing a book about the robe of Jesus and it will be called *The Arriving of the King.* Andrew did not know about this book before God showed this to him in Heaven. *The Arriving of the King* is about a vision that I saw during our worship service at Living Word Revival Center, the color of the robe of Jesus was mainly red satin with a 4 inch purple satin trim with a long train. That is why Andrew saw the book red and purple; please reference this scripture to validate the color of his robe. And I saw heaven opened, and behold a white horse; and he that sat upon him was called Faithful and True, and in righteousness he doth judge and make war. His eyes were as a flame of fire, and on his head were many crowns; and he had a name written, that no man knew, but he himself. And he was clothed with a vesture dipped in blood: and his name is called The Word of God.[161] And the soldiers platted a crown of thorns, and put it on his head, and they put on him a purple robe. And said, *"Hail, King of the Jews!"* And they smote him with their hands.[162] There is more information on the robe of Jesus that will be included with my book *The Arriving of the King*! God told the prophet Daniel, "But thou, O Daniel, shut up the words, and seal the book, even to the time of the end: many shall run to and fro, and knowledge shall be increased.[163] God loves to confirm his word. *How many books were in the library Andrew?*

Andrew: There were sections from A to Z with millions and billions of books in them! Then there would be this room that had a gold door knob, and then the door was just a regular door. You open the door, but on the top of the door it would have one of those things that would say something, like a title on a door it said, *Grand Books*. But when you'd walk in there the first time it would have one book. It would say, all that the person's done this and that.

Mom: I love to write about what God places in my spirit, I have many books and songs that I have written, and they are kept for such a time as when God says to release them. I love to gain wisdom and knowledge and the best way to do that is to read God's word and then go before God and he will reveal his spirit of knowledge and understanding to you.[164] *What do you mean; all the person's done this and that?*

Andrew: It was like you are the keeper of what happened and stuff. Like if people hit their sister or something like that it would say that. And if they didn't do that, it would be erased automatically by God. You are like this famous author in Heaven.

Mom: So it seems as if I will serve God writing down things that God tells me to write down that happen on the earth, and when a person asks for forgiveness God will erase that action, I will do whatever God instructs me to do in Heaven! *So in the grand room, was a room I had books in?*

Andrew: Yes, you had books in there: Then it would be like if the devil would try to get in there he wouldn't be able to get in there. When you go into that room it would have like a shield, he can't even get into your house or library. He can't even get through the gate. He'd try to but if he did, he'd probably get obliviated. When you went into that room, it smelled like marshmallows, it would smell really good, and when you'd read the books you would never want to stop reading them. Heaven was really good.

Mom: Satan has been banished from Heaven for eternity so we know that he will never be able to return to Heaven, God banished Satan and a third of the angels because they wanted to control all of Heaven and take God's place. *God is the great I am and no one can take God's place! What were the books about?*

Andrew: All about God, and what people had done. Another book that you wrote was called, *Lucifer's Attacks!*

Mom: I have considered writing a book on *Lucifer's Attacks,* looks like I will need to start this one I have a lot to write to you about this topic. *You said that doorknob had a "J" on it?*

Andrew: Yes, it stands for Jesus. When you go to Heaven the streets would be all gold. The sidewalks, they'd be like diamonds. And when you'd fall, you wouldn't be hurt. When you went swimming you could breathe underwater. Even, you wouldn't be afraid because no one would attack you. It would be like the perfect place. You are surrounded by people who would not hurt you. All they would do is help you out. It was like they were your best friend and you didn't even know them on earth. You'd probably be saying, "Why did I not know them?" I also saw a stable with the manger that the baby Jesus was in, and there were a lot of animals there too. Then there was a palace that I knew was God's palace and every gold road in Heaven led to the palace. The palace was larger than any of the other buildings in Heaven; it was gold, with different colored jewels on it, but mostly gold. The top of this palace was pointed like a pyramid is. The streets of gold were very wide. I didn't go into the palace because God really wanted me to see your gold mansion. However, I am asking God to take me back to Heaven so I can see the inside of his palace!

Mom: We know how important names are we can see from the word of God that particular attention is placed on the names of families. There is no other name like the name of Jesus I love the detail on the doorknob with the letter "J" on it!!! I love the streets of gold that Andrew talks about; there is reference

in the word of God that states this about the gold streets in
Heaven, *"And the twelve gates were twelve pearls: every several
gate was of one pearl: and the street of the city was pure gold, as
it were transparent glass."*[165] Also, imagine the sidewalks that
glisten they are made of diamonds! There is no pain in Heaven
if you do fall down, and I think it is so great that we will be
able to breathe underwater. Oh I can only imagine the beauty
and splendor of the fish, and the reefs underwater, I bet there
are also mansions underwater, image an entire city underwater! I can't wait to meet everyone in Heaven and listen to
their experiences! I know what Andrew means when he says it
was like they were your best friend and you didn't know them
on earth. I had this experience once when my husband and I
were in Bogota, Colombia with Apostles Steven and Valerie
Swisher. We were at this huge conference of about 5,000 people and when the conference was over we were escorted to
an area to meet some of the people who were serving in the
house of the Lord. The word of God tells us that you will
know them by the spirit, or otherwise by the fruit, because the
fruit of the spirit is love.[166] There was this lady that I met she
only spoke Spanish and I only spoke English, so you would
think with the language barrier that we would not be able to
understand each other, well when I saw her and she saw me
it was like Andrew said, it was like they were your best friend,
she smiled and so did I and I saw the word *JOY* in bold capital
letters to my left in the spirit that God was communicating
with me to impart to her. So, I prayed over her and just spoke
the *JOY* of the Lord over her well she just started laughing
and so did I and then everyone around us started to laugh too.
Every good father knows how important it is for their children to laugh! I just had this feeling that I knew her forever,
just like you know a best friend. God loves to keep records
of everything that happens in this world, no wonder Andrew

would see the stable with the manger that his son Jesus laid in at his birth here in this world, along with the animals. The top of the palace that Andrew saw was shaped like a pyramid, but was squared off on one side. Andrew said that every gold road in Heaven led to the palace. All roads do lead straight to Jesus think about this for a moment, when you die one day you will face Jesus on judgment day and he will judge you on how you have lived the life that he gave you to live here on this earth. Have you accepted Jesus as your Lord and Savior? Are you born again, being baptized receiving the Holy Spirit? Have you read the Holy Bible that contains God's word and applied his word to your life? Some people think because they are *good* people that they will go to Heaven this is just not true. What is your definition of *good?* Now, what is Jesus' definition of *good?* Read God's word, have a desire to know him he is your creator. You are made in his image; "*So God created man in his own image, in the image of God created he him; male and female he created he them.*"[167] Declare Jesus as Lord of your life today. Jesus has given us his words of life, and when you apply them to your life you will live eternally in Heaven with God and his angels, in your beautiful mansion, eternal peace and tranquility, and every desire God loves to bestow gifts on his children, however if you are an unbeliever and choose not to follow Jesus you will spend eternity in Hell with Satan and his demons, an eternal damnation where there is no rest, no water, extreme heart, sorrow and pain I could go on but I believe that you understand the picture that I am explaining to you here. Jesus will either send you to Heaven or to Hell there are only two places to choose from. Jesus saith unto him, "*I am the way, the truth, and the life: no man cometh unto the Father, but by me. If ye had known me, ye should have known my Father also: and from henceforth ye know him, and have seen him.*"[168]

I would like to take this moment and decree over your life that God is opening your eyes to see and ears to hear him through dreams and visions that are from the God. As these dreams and visions begin to unfold upon your life, you will begin to see who God is in your life and who you are to him. For you are a royal priesthood, you are a chosen generation, follow the talents that God has given you always seeking him diligently and God will show you which direction to take. God will bless your life in such a mighty way when you walk in the talents that he has placed upon your life. You are an overcomer, you are chosen for this time, and we are walking in the latter day's march forward knowing that God will supply all of your needs. Never looking back at your past, always looking forward with your eyes focused upon God. God is smiling down upon you even now, for he sees your heart is for him and he loves you so very much. I thank God for you and I know that as you walk in God's will for your life, there will be other people that will step into the talents that God has created for their lives. We are to walk in love and unity following the example of Jesus, and we are more than conquers through Jesus. We have overcome by the blood of the lamb. Shout out your testimony for the glory of God, and always remember to thank God for everything in your life. I thank you God for the person that is reading this right now, I thank you for placing this teaching within their hands and I thank you God for restoration upon their life. I decree that they will come to know you in a greater measure and that by coming to know you in that deeper way, they find you and they find out who they are through you. Glory to God in the highest! Amen!

EPILOGUE

In conclusion, I wrote this book for many reasons and here is a recap why. When I began this journey with God, he took me from Hell's fire and gave me a chance to repent for all of the anger I had towards him. Let's just stop here for a moment, Jesus Christ, King of Kings and Lord of Lords, loves me so much that he took time to speak with me, that moment still brings me to tears, I am crying right now as I am writing this to you. Sin cannot stand in the presence of Jesus for the light of his love burns out every sin that dwells within you. I can imagine the day that I stand before Jesus once again, I will not be able to for his love has brought me to my knees, declaring he is the Lord of my life, I humble myself before him asking him, Lord have I walked in your love today towards others? Please find me worthy to spend eternity in Heaven with you my Lord. I chose to swallow my foolish pride the day Jesus walked into my life, I repented of my sin that was against him, for he was not the reason why my babies died, he was the reason they were alive in Heaven. At that moment Jesus forgave me instantly and I was handed the keys to enter into the *Gates of Heaven* by opening my eyes to see who God is to me and who I am in the Kingdom of God. As I drew closer to God he began to reveal more of his heart to me. Speaking to me daily through dreams and visions I began to write down every single dream and vision and took time with God to understand what he was saying to me. When you take time out of your day and trust in God he will open up doors in your life and pour out blessings that are overflowing into your life. I began to go over my journals that I kept with dreams and visions and I began to see these dreams and visions come true. I would go back to find that one particular dream or vision from God and I was able to see what God was doing in my life. God is so amazing my life was unfolding right before my eyes and God had already revealed this to me. I know that God has a sense of humor because dressing me up in a *Little Bo Peep* outfit definitely opened my eyes to see who God was calling me to be for the Kingdom of God. When God told me *"feed my sheep"* and handed me the beautiful staff I had a choice at that moment as well to either grab the staff or not, I chose to obey and grabbed the staff, declaring my love for Jesus. Jesus told me *feed my sheep* for when we *feed his sheep* Jesus knows that we truly love him. We read about this when Jesus challenges Peter, after Jesus has resurrected from the dead. Refer to this experience for wisdom, this is now the third time that Jesus shewed himself to the disciples, after that he was risen from the dead. So when they dined, Jesus saith to Simon Peter, *"Simon, son of Jonas, lovest thou me more than these?"* He saith unto him, *"Yea Lord; thou knowest that I love thee."* He saith unto him, *"Feed my lambs."* He saith to him again the second time, *"Simon, son of Jonas, lovest thou me?"* He saith unto him, *"Yea, Lord; thou knowest that I love thee."* He saith unto him, *"Feed my sheep."* He saith unto him the third time, *"Simon, son of Jonas, lovest thou me?"* And he said unto him, *"Lord thou knowest all things; thou knowest that I love thee."* Jesus saith unto him, *"Feed my sheep."*[169] Jesus *called me* to *feed his sheep*, and *I chose to accept the call to show my love for Jesus.* Seeing the huge football stadium without a ceiling was a breathtaking experience, opening my eyes to see that there are many people waiting to hear *God's word,* and those people are waiting for me to realize who I am. Now I know who I am, I am an *Evangelist* that has accepted the call to *feed God's sheep with his word,* going to the nations, declaring my love for Jesus to the world!

As I began to mediate on the word of God listening to praise and worship music spending time with God one on one, I began to build my personal relationship with God. I would praise the Lord and worship the Lord in spirit and truth, God began to sing over me and I began to write what God was speaking with me, the words just flowed from the pen onto the paper, God was releasing his heart to me and songs were created from start to finish, lyrics and melody. There are so many songs that God has released to me, I would ask God why are there so many God. God's response to me was this, *"There are so many because I love you, and I am singing over you, in time you will use these songs for my glory. Continue to write the songs that I release to you for the glory of the Lord is shining upon you."* So, I would take time and write these songs down and I bought a keyboard and began to peck one note out at a time, because I could hear the melody that God released, I would record my worship times with God, this way I could remember the words and the melody. I would like to share with you a season that I went through as God was releasing his songs of love over my life. There was a time period where I thought the songs that God had given to me were not *good enough* to share with everyone. I was comparing myself with other people and the songs that they had written. As I came before the Lord one day sharing this with him this was his reply to me, *"I have released my heart to you, and what I have released to you is my will for you, if you continue to judge the songs that I place within your life as not good enough to release in your life when I tell you to, I will stop releasing songs to you. For the songs that I have placed upon your life are for your life and for the life of others as well, release the songs that I have given to you and you will see the fruit of this talent manifest for this work is not in vain, this work is for my glory, for you to release upon this dry and thirsty world."* Okay, Lord understand, I am sorry that

I judged the songs that you have given to me as not *good enough,* I will continue to persevere knowing that you have a plan for my life, and I will not let other people direct my steps Lord I will follow only you. So, as my relationship with God grew deeper, dreams and visions began to invade my days and nights and as I studied what God revealed to me in symbols, I was able to understand how God talks with me and why he talks with me in this way. Please refer to this statement that Jesus declared in reference to why he speaks in parables with us, *"Therefore speak I to them in parables: because they seeing see not; and hearing they hear not, neither do they understand. And in them is fulfilled the prophecy of Esaias, which saith, By hearing ye shall hear, and shall not understand; and seeing ye shall see, and shall not perceive: For this people's heart is waxed gross, and their ears are dull of hearing, and their eyes they have closed; lest any time they should see with their eyes, and hear with their ears, and should understand with their heart, and should be converted, and I should heal them. But blessed are your eyes, for they see: and your ears, for they hear. For verily, I say unto you, That many prophets and righteous men have desired to see those things which ye hear, and have not heard them. Hear ye therefore the parable of the sower. When any one heareth the word of the kingdom, and understandeth it not, then cometh the wicked one, and catcheth away that which was sown in his heart. This is he which receiveth seed by the way side. But he that received the seed into stony places, the same is he that heareth the word and anon with joy receiveth it; Ye hath he not root in himself, but dureth for awhile; for when tribulation or persecution ariseth because of the word, by and by his is offended. He also that received seed among the thorns is he that heareth the word; and the care of this world and deceitfulness of riches, choke the word, and becometh unfruitful. But he that received the seed into the good ground is he that heareth my word, and understandeth it; which also beareth fruit, and bringeth forth, some an hundredfold, some sixty, some thirty."*[170] The seed is the word of God, and as you receive understanding of the word of God you are standing on the foundation of God which is his word. Everything that God has created is spoken by his voice, Jesus is the word. Thus why Jesus tells us this, *"I am the way, the truth, and the life: no man cometh unto the Father, but by me. If ye had known me, ye should have known my Father also: and from henceforth ye know him, and have seen him."*[171] Let us no longer be *frozen in our flesh,* the time is now for the bride of Jesus Christ to arise and shine for the glory of the Lord is risen upon you! You are a mighty warrior for the Kingdom of God and God will never leave you or forsake you, for you belong to him. As I saw my bride dress in Heaven I was able to see the many obstacles that I had overcome, and God gave me the desire of my heart that I prayed to him. For he tells us to ask and we shall receive. You see God already knows what we need; however, we need to rely on God to fulfill his purpose for our life. God is our foundation and when we are grounded in his word and rely on him to fulfill these desires he will do it. You can do it!!! You are an overcomer through Jesus Christ!!! Remember the teaching about the Challah bread; the Lord told me to remind you of this again, *"Continue to pursue me diligently with all of your mind, soul, heart and physical strength. Taste and see that the Lord is good, for you can't make a loaf of Challah bread without these ingredients if you are missing one it will not be the same."* Let the love of Jesus fill your heart and spill over onto those who you come into contact with. We can change this world one person at a time, and as we begin to walk in unity we begin to see Jesus is the bread of life and that he will stir the hearts of those that we meet all we need to do is plant that seed and watch the seed grow. The seed is the word of God, and think of the mustard seed my friend, it is such a tiny seed when you look at it, however when you plant that seed it becomes a very large tree. So take that step of faith and see yourself planting that seed of faith, watering it every day with the spirit of the Lord for that seed is planted in great soil the foundation is the infallible word of God, hence where man came from for God created man from the dust of the earth, breathing life into him to walk with him in the garden of Eden. You are destined for eternity in Heaven with God!

You will begin to see Heaven invading this earth, as your relationship with God grows deeper understanding him. Remember when I saw the iridescent pink angel feather in my right shoe the next morning after the warning dream from God, that feather confirmed the word of God giving me a boldness to move forward. God loves to confirm his word and God will manifest his presence in many different ways upon our lives, it is our choice or will to see those moments that God gives to us. Is seeing an angel believing that God will manifest his presence to you? Surely not for God is always with us, even when we think we are alone we are not, God is always with us. God assigns a guardian angel to us and that angel helps us to walk out the call that God has placed upon our lives. So when we are crying out to God for help, he will send our guardian angel, and other angels to help guide us they are his messengers. God manifests his presence to you every moment of every day, just look around this earth that he made for you and I to dwell in, this earth is beautiful and God created this earth for us to live in. When I declared over my life, *"Oh, God that you would bless me and enlarge my territory,"* God answered back telling me that I would have a son and his name would be called Isaac. I know I heard the audible voice of God speaking this to me. Know this, Satan will try to steal the seed that God gives to you, after I heard this word from the Lord I became pregnant about a year later. I was three months into this pregnancy and I had another miscarriage. This would be my third miscarriage. However, at this stage in my relationship with God I did not blame him, I thanked him for loving me so much that he would take care of this baby and when I walked through the gates of Heaven I would see all of the babies that are in Heaven. The

Lord told me to name every baby that I miscarried, the first one is Gabriel, the second is Angelica and the third one is Mark. Satan tried to deceive me into calling the third baby I miscarried Isaac, he tried to steal the promise that God had already spoken into my life. I named the third baby after my guardian angel Mark. Mark has surely defended me through several attacks from Satan and I was not going to let Satan steal God's promise over my life, for God has a purpose for Isaac and I know that God is faithful. Three years after God spoke into my life that I would have son and name him Isaac, the word of God came true, the child of promise over my life entered this world in God's timing, filling this world with the laughter of God.

God's timing is always perfect and that is why God took my 10 year old son Andrew to Hell and to Heaven while I was in the process of reformatting this book to be published. God wanted Andrew to experience Hell and Heaven catapulting Andrew into his calling of the *Evangelist.* Andrew understood Hell in a totally new way. Within this understanding God released a fire in Andrew's belly that allowed the river of God to flow from his mouth. Andrew could never imagine me in Hell because he loves me so much. However, God spoke with Andrew and told him that this was where his mom would have been if she did not repent for placing blame on God for the loss of her children. This dream sparked a passion to save the world and to *feed God's sheep* because of his love for God. Ironically, both my son Andrew and I share the same office in the Kingdom of God, the *Evangelist.* During Andrew's dream of Heaven, God shared with him secret's that were between only God and I. Such as my favorite color being turquoise, the writing of another book called, *"The Arriving of the King."* God released this information to Andrew because God needed to confirm what Andrew had heard from God as the truth, for only I knew those things and had not shared them with anyone. When Andrew spoke of my gold mansion in

Heaven he spoke in such an enthusiasm at how great my mansion in Heaven is. In the song, *"The Gates of Heaven,"* there is a line where I say, *"I see a great mansion for me,"* now I know that my mansion is gold and a lot of details about my mansion and my library and the grand room. When Andrew heard me sing that line he said to me, *"Mom, you have no idea, your mansion is truly great!"* When Andrew spoke these words to me his words pierced my heart. I began to think again about the love of God, and all of the blessings that God has bestowed upon my life. To know that God has more for me to receive and experience for eternity when I enter into the gates of Heaven, is truly his love for me. I thank you God for all of the blessings that you have blessed me with in my life.

It is my prayer to God that in writing this book that you will have a greater understanding of who God is in your life opening your eyes to who God has called you to be in your lifetime, seeking a closer relationship with God through this teaching. I would love to hear your testimonies feel free to email me at sherryconrad@ live.com. If you need advice in discerning a dream or vision please email me and I will get back in touch with you. Join my Facebook group, "God's Insight For Your Life Through Dreams And Visions" where we discuss dreams and visions. God bless you abundantly, Sherry.

Symbolic dictionary based on God's word the Holy Bible (KJV).

ALL LIVING CREATURES GREAT & SMALL

An important fact to keep in mind is that when you have a dream or vision and your personal pet is within the dream or vision, this will directly pertain to your personal pet as being your loyal friend.

Adder/Viper (Deadly/Gossip): They have sharpened their tongues like a serpent; adders' poison is under their lips. Selah (Psalm 140:3). (Also see **Serpent**)

Ant (Wise): Go to the ant, thou sluggard; consider her ways, and be wise: Which having no guide, overseer, or ruler, provideth her meat in the summer, gathereth her food in the harvest (Proverbs 6:6-8).

Bat (Idol worship): And they shall go into the holes of the rocks, and into the caves of the earth, for fear of the Lord, and for the glory of his majesty, when he ariseth to shake terribly the earth. In that day a man shall cast his idols of silver, and his idols of gold, which they made each one to himself to worship, to the moles and to the bats (Isaiah 2:19-21).

Bear (Devourer of the Flesh who is Satan/Wicked Ruler): And behold another beast, a second, like to a bear, and it raised up itself on one side, and it had three ribs in the mouth of it between the teeth of it: and they said thus unto it, Arise, devour much flesh (Daniel 7:5). As a roaring lion, and a ranging bear; so is a wicked ruler over the poor people (Proverbs 28:15).

Bees (Attack/Gossip/To Swarm):(Attack): And the Amorites, which dwelt in that mountain, came out against you, and chased you, as bees do, and destroyed you in Seir, even unto Hormah (Deuteronomy 1:44).

(Gossip): And withal they learn to be idle, wandering about from house to house; and not only idle, but tattlers also and busybodies, speaking things which they ought not (1 Timothy 5:13).

(To Swarm): They compassed me like bees; they are quenched as the fire of thorns: for in the name of the Lord I will destroy them (Psalm 118:12).

Behemoth/Hippopotamus (Swift & Strong Elder/Laborer): Then will I also confess unto thee that thine own right hand can save thee. Behold now behemoth, which I made with thee; he eateth grass as an ox. Lo now, his strength is in his loins, and his force is in the navel of his belly (Job 40:14-16).

Birds (See Crow, Dove, Eagle, Owl and Raven)

Black Horse (Drought/Famine): And when he had opened the third seal, I heard the third beast say, *"Come and see."* And I beheld, and lo a black horse; and he that sat on him had a pair of balances in his hand. And I heard a voice in the midst of the four beasts say, *"A measure of wheat for a penny, and three measures of barley for a penny; and see thou hurt not the oil and the wind (Revelation 6: 5-6)."*

Bull (Fierce & Relentless Adversaries): Thy sons have fainted; they lie at the head of all the streets, as a wild bull in a net: they are full of fury of the Lord, the rebuke of thy God (Isaiah 51:20).

Camel (Servanthood/Bearing the burdens of others): And Isaac came from the way of the well Lahairoi; for he dwelt in the south country. And Isaac went out to meditate in the field at the eventide: and he lifted up his eyes, and saw, and, behold, the camels were coming. And Rebekah lifted up her eyes, and when she saw Isaac, she lighted off the camel (Genesis 24:62-64).

Cankerworm/Caterpillar/Locust/Palmerworm (Good/Restoration from the devourer of men) Be glad then, ye children of Zion, and rejoice in the Lord your God: for he hath given you the former rain moderately, and he will cause to come down for you the rain, the former rain, and the latter rain in the first month. And the floors shall be full of wheat, and the vats shall overflow with wine and oil. And I will restore to you the years that the locust hath eaten, the cankerworm, my great army which I sent among you. And ye shall eat in plenty, and be satisfied and praise the name of the Lord you God, that hath dealt wondrously with you: and my people shall never be ashamed. And ye shall know that I am in the midst of Israel, and that I am the Lord your God, and none else: and my people shall never be ashamed (Joel 2:23-27).

(Evil/Devourer of Men without the seal of God in their foreheads): And the fifth angel sounded, and I saw a star fall from heaven unto the earth: and to him was given the key of the bottomless pit. And he opened the bottomless pit; and there arose a smoke out of the pit, as the smoke of a great furnace: and the sun and the air were darkened by reason of smoke of the pit. And there came out of the smoke locusts upon the earth: and unto them was given power, as the scorpions of the earth have power. And it was commanded them that they should not hurt the grass of the earth, neither any green thing, neither any tree; but only those men which have not the seal of God in their foreheads. And to them it was given that they should not kill them, but that they should be tormented five month: and their torment was the torment of a scorpion, when he striketh a man. And in those days shall men seek death, and shall not find it; and shall desire to die, and death shall flee from them. And the shapes of the locusts were like unto horses prepared for battle; and on their heads were as it were crowns like gold, and their faces were as the faces of men. And they had hair as the hair of women, and their teeth were as the teeth of lions. And they had breastplates, as it were breastplates of iron; and the sound of chariots of many horses running to battle. And they had tails like unto scorpions, and there were stings in their tails; and their power was to hurt men five months. And they had a king over them, which is the angel of the bottomless pit, whose name is Abaddon, but in the Greek tongue has his name Apollyon. One woe is past; and, behold, there come two woes more hereafter (Revelation 9:1-12).

FYI: The locust suddenly appear in great numbers devouring herbage, however the above scriptures state that the angel said that they were not to touch the herbage and only the men who do not have the seal of God in their foreheads meaning those who are serving Satan (Abaddon) there flesh will be eaten and they will wish for death and death will not come, stop walking in your flesh, ask God to forgive you of your sins, declare Jesus as the son of God and as your Savior and enter the Gates of Heaven!

Cat (See Leopard and Lion)

Cow (Prosperity/Milk/Meat/Sacrifice): And Abram was very rich in cattle, in silver, and in gold (Genesis 13:2).

Crocodile (Idolatry): Professing themselves to be wise, they became fools, and changed the glory of the uncorruptible God into an image made like to a corruptible man, and to birds, and fourfooted beasts, and creeping things (Romans 1:23).

Crow/Raven/Birds (God's messenger of provision/Birds singing for Jesus has come to rapture his bride/Satan stealing the word of God): *"And it shall be, that thou shalt drink of the brook; and I have commanded the ravens to feed thee there."* So he went and did according unto the word of the Lord: for he went and dwelt by the brook Cherith, that is before Jordan. And the ravens brought him bread and flesh in the morning, and bread and flesh in the evening; and he drank of the brook (1 Kings 17:4-6).

(Birds singing a new song Jesus has come to rapture his bride): *"For, lo, the winter is past, the rain is over and gone; The flowers appear on the earth; the time of the singing of birds is come, and the voice of the turtle is heard in our land; The fig tree putteth forth her green figs, and the vines with the tender grape give a good smell. Arise, my love, my fair one, and come away (Song of Solomon 2:11-13)."*

(Satan stealing the word of God): And he spake many things unto them in parables, saying, *"Behold, a sower went forth to sow; And when he sowed, some seeds fell by the way side, and the fowls came and devoured them up (Mathew 13:3-4)."*

Dove (Holy Spirit): And I knew him not: but that he should be made manifest to Israel, therefore am I come baptizing with water. And John bare record, saying, I saw the Spirit descending from heaven like a dove, and it abode upon him. And I knew him not: but he that sent me to baptize with water, the same said unto me, upon whom shalt see the Spirit descending, and remaining on him, the same is he which baptizeth with the Holy Ghost. And I saw, and bare record that this is the Son of God (John 1:31-34).

Dog (To Return to Sin/Habit): As a dog returneth to his vomit, so a fool returneth to his folly (Proverbs 26:11).

FYI: Dogs eat their vomit and feces to hide signs of their presence from predators. God is always watching us and will see our sin it can't be hidden.

Donkey (God made the donkey talk to Balaam to stop his impending death): And the ass said unto Balaam, *"Am not I thine ass, upon which thou hast ridden ever since I was thine unto this day? was I ever wont to do so unto thee?"* and he said, *"Nay."* Then the Lord opened the eyes of Balaam, and he saw the angel of the Lord standing in the way, and his sword drawn in his hand: and he bowed down his head, and fell flat on his face. And the angel of the Lord said unto him, *"Wherefore hast thou smitten thine ass these three times? behold, I went out to withstand thee, because thy way is perverse before me: And the ass saw me, and turned from me these three times: unless she had turned from me, surely now also I had slain thee, and saved her alive."* And Balaam said unto the angel of the Lord, *I have sinned; for I knew not that thou stoodest in the way against me: now therefore, if it displease thee, I will get me back again.* And the angel of the Lord said unto Balaam, *"Go with the men: but only the word that I shall speak unto thee, that thou shalt speak (Numbers 22:30-35)."*

Dragon/Red Dragon (Satan): And the great dragon was cast out, that old serpent, called the Devil, and Satan, which deceiveth the whole world: he was cast out into the earth, and his angels were cast out with him (Revelation 12:9).

(Red Dragon/Satan): And there appeared another wonder in heaven; and behold a great red dragon, having seven heads and ten horns, and seven crowns upon his heads. And his tail drew the third part of the stars of heaven, and did cast them to the earth: and the dragon stood before the woman which was ready to be delivered, for to devour her child as soon as it was born (Revelation 12:3-4).

Eagle (Leader/Prophet "Eagle Eye"/God's Strength): Ye have seen what I did unto the Egyptians, and how I bare you on eagles' wings, and brought you unto myself (Exodus 19:4).

As an eagle stirreth up her nest, fluttereth over her young, spreadeth abroad her wings, taketh them, beareth them on her wings (Deuteronomy 32:11).

But they that wait upon the Lord shall renew their strength; they shall mount up with wings as eagles; they shall run, and not be weary; and they shall walk, and not faint (Isaiah 40:31).

Fish (Dolphins, Sharks and other types of fish fall into this category) (All of Mankind): *"Again, the kingdom of heaven is like unto a net, that was cast into the sea, and gathered of every kind: Which when it was full, they drew to shore, and sat down, and gathered the good into vessels, but cast the bad away. So shall it be at the end of the world: the angels shall come forth, and sever the wicked from among the just. And shall cast them into the furnaces of fire: there shall be wailing and gnashing of teeth."* Jesus saith unto them, *"Have ye understood all these things?"* They said unto him, *"Yea, Lord."* Then said he unto them, *"Therefore every scribe which is instructed unto the kingdom of heaven is like unto a man that is a householder, which brings forth out of his treasure things new and old (Mathew 13:47-52)."*

Flea (Not important to pursue): After whom is the king of Israel come out? After whom dost thou pursue? After a dead dog, after a flea (1 Samuel 24:14).

Flies (Unclean): And the Lord did so; and there came a grievous swarm of flies into the house of Pharaoh, and into his servants' houses, and into all the land of Egypt: the land was corrupted by reason of the swarm of flies (Exodus 8:24).

Fox (False Prophet): Take us the foxes, the little foxes that spoil the vines: for our vines have tender grapes (Song of Solomon 2:15).

Frog (Demonic Spirit): And I saw three unclean spirits like frogs come out of the mouth of the dragon, and out of the mouth of the beast, and out of the mouth of the false prophet (Revelation 16:13).

Goat (Sinners): When the Son of man shall come in his glory, and all the holy angels with him, then shall he sit upon the throne of his glory: and before him shall be gathered all nations: and he shall separate them one from another, as a shepherd divideth his sheep from the goats: And he shall set the sheep on his right hand, but the goats on the left (Mathew 25:31-33).

FYI: Sheep are docile, gentle creatures, but goats are unruly and rambunctious and can easily upset the sheep. They do not feed or rest well together, so the shepherd separates them for grazing and for sleeping at night. When the Lord Jesus Christ returns he will separate believers from unbelievers to establish His millennial kingdom. He will put the believing sheep on his right, the place of favor and blessing, and the unbelieving goats on the left, the place of disfavor and rejection.

Hen (God's protection): *"Verily I say unto you, all these things shall come upon this generation. O Jerusalem, Jerusalem, thou that killest the prophets, and stonest them which are sent unto thee, how often would I have gathered thy children together, even as a hen gathereth her chickens under her wings, and ye would not! Behold, your house is left unto you desolate (Mathew 23:36-38)."*

Hornet/Wasp (God used his creation to drive the enemy out): *"And I sent the hornet before you, which drave them out from before you, even the two kings of the Amorites; but not with thy sword, nor with thy bow (Joshua 24:12)."*

Horse (God's swift powerful ministry): *"Behold, he shall come up as the clouds, and his chariots shall be as a whirlwind: his horses are swifter than eagles. Woe unto us! For we are spoiled (Jeremiah 4:13)."*

Lamb/Sheep (Jesus is the Lamb of God/Children of God are his sheep/Children without a Shepherd): He was oppressed, and he was afflicted, yet he opened not his mouth: he is brought as a lamb to the slaughter, and as a sheep before her shearers is dumb, so he openeth not his mouth (Isaiah 53:7).

　　The next day John seeth Jesus coming unto him, and saith, *"Behold the Lamb of God, which taketh away the sin of the world (John 1:29)."*

(Children of God are his sheep): My sheep hear my voice, and I know them, and they follow me (John 10:27).

(Children without a shepherd): And Jesus, when he came out, saw much people, and was moved with compassion toward them, because they were as sheep not having a shepherd: and he began to teach them many things (Mark 6:34).

FYI: The lamb and the sheep are the same animal however; a lamb is a sheep that is 12 months old or less. The word lamb is used to describe the lamb's meat. When a lamb becomes a year old it is referred to as a sheep.

Leopard (God/Good/Satan/Evil): (God/Good): Wherefore a lion out of the forest shall slay them, and a wolf of the evenings shall spoil them, a leopard shall watch over their cities: every one that goeth out thence shall be torn in pieces: because their transgressions are many, and their backslidings are increased (Jeremiah 5:6).

(Satan/Evil): After this I beheld, and lo another, like a leopard, which had upon the back of it four wings of a fowl; the beast had also four heads; and dominion was given to it (Daniel 7:6).

Leviathan (Gatekeeper of Hell/Satan): In that day the Lord with his sore and great and strong sword shall punish leviathan the piercing serpent, even leviathan that crooked serpent; and he shall slay the dragon that is in the sea (Isaiah 27:1).

Lion (Christ/Good): And one of the elders saith unto me, *"Weep not: behold, the Lion of the tribe of Juda, the Root of David, hath prevailed to open the book, and to loose the seven seals thereof. And I beheld, and, lo, in the midst of the throne and of the four beasts, and in the midst of the elders, stood a Lamb as it had been slain, having seven horns and seven eyes, which are the seven Spirits of God sent forth into all the earth (Revelation 5:5-6)."*

FYI: And there shall come forth a rod out of the stem of Jesse, and a Branch shall grow out of his roots: And the spirit of the Lord shall rest upon him, the spirit of wisdom and understanding, the spirit of counsel and might, the spirit of knowledge and the fear of the Lord. And shall make him of quick understanding in the fear of the Lord: and he shall not judge after the sight of his eyes, neither reprove after the hearing of his ears: but with righteousness shall he judge the poor, and reprove with equity for the meek of the earth: and he shall smite the earth with the rod of his mouth, and with the breath of his lips shall he slay the wicked. And the righteousness shall be the girdle of his loins, and faithfulness the girdle of his reins (Isaiah 11:1-5). The Seven Spirits of God are Wisdom, Understanding, Counsel, Might, Knowledge, Righteousness and the Fear of the Lord.

(Satan/Evil): *"Humble yourselves therefore under the mighty hand of God, that he may exalt you in due time: casting all your care upon him; for he careth for you. Be sober, be vigilant; because your adversary the devil, as a roaring lion, walketh about; seeking whom he may devour: whom resist stedfast in the faith, knowing that the same afflictions are accomplished in your brethren that are in the world (1 Peter 5:6-9)."*

Locusts (See Cankerworm/Caterpillar/Locust/Palmerworm)

Mice (Pestilence/Bubonic Plague): Then said they, *"What shall be the trespass offering which we shall return to him?"* They answered, *"Five golden emerods, and five golden mice, according to the number of the lords of the Philistines: for one plague was on you all, and on your lords (1 Samuel 6:4)."*

Molten Calf (Idolatry): And the Lord said unto Moses, *"Go get thee down; for thy people, which thou broughtest out of the land of Egypt, have corrupted themselves, they have turned aside quickly out of the way which I commanded them; they have made them a molten calf, and have worshipped it, and have sacrificed thereunto,* and said, *"These be thy gods, O Israel, which have brought thee up out of the land of Egypt"* and the Lord said unto Moses, *"I have seen this people, and, behold, it is a stiffnecked people (Exodus 32:7-9)."*

Mule (Stiff-necked): *"Be ye not as the horse, or as the mule, which have no understanding; whose mouth must be held in with bit and bridle, lest they come near unto thee (Psalm 32:9)."*

Owl (Evil/Sin/Idolatry): There shall the great owl make her nest, and lay, and hatch, and gather under her shadow; there shall the vultures also be gathered, everyone with her mate (Isaiah 34:15).

(Sin): I went mourning without the sun: I stood up, and I cried in the congregation. I am a brother to dragons, and a companion to owls. My skin is black upon me, and my bones are burned with heat (Job 30:28-30).

(Idolatry): They shall call the nobles thereof to the kingdom, but none shall be there, and all her princes shall be nothing. And thorns shall come up in her palaces, nettles and brambles in the fortresses thereof: and it shall be an habitation of dragons, and a court for owls. The wild beasts of the desert shall also meet with the wild beasts of the island, and the satyr shall cry to his fellow; the screech owl also shall rest there, and find for herself a place of rest (Isaiah 34:12-14).

Ostrich/Peacock (Lacking Wisdom/Vain/Not thankful for the blessings that God gives): Gavest thou the godly wings unto the peacocks? Or wings and feathers unto the ostrich? Which leaveth her eggs in the earth, and warmeth them in dust. And forgetteth that the foot may crush them, or that the wild beast may break them. She is hardened against her young ones, as though they were not hers: her labour is in vain without fear; because God hath deprived her of wisdom, neither hath he imparted to her understanding. What time she lifteth up herself on high, she scorneth the horse and his rider (Job 39:12-18).

FYI: The ostrich and the peacock are spoken of in these scriptures as walking without the wisdom and understanding of the blessings that God has given them in their life which are their children. It is obvious that they are not taking care of their young ones and they are being crushed by the enemy. God has given you your children as a blessing, be an example to your children by following God so that your children will follow God too, for if you do not Satan will take them.

Ox (Elder/Laborer): *"Let the elders that rule well be counted worthy of double honour, especially they who labour in the word and doctrine."* For the scripture saith, *"Thou shalt not muzzle the ox that treadeth out the corn. And, the labourer is worthy of his reward. Against an elder receive not an accusation, but before two or three witnesses (1 Timothy 5:18)."*

Pale Horse (Death): *"And I looked, and behold a pale horse: and his name that sat on him was Death, and Hell followed with him. And power was given unto them over the fourth part of the earth, to kill with sword, and with hunger, and with death, and with the beasts of the earth (Revelation 6:8)."*

Raven (God's messenger used for provision/as Judgement for dishonoring your father and mother): *"And it shall be that thou shalt drink of the brook; and I have commanded the ravens to feed thee there."* So he went and did according unto the word of the Lord: for he went and dwelt by the brook Cherith that is before Jordan. And the ravens brought him bread and flesh in the morning, and bread and flesh in the evening; and he drank of the brook (1 Kings 17: 4-6).

The eye that mocketh at his father, and despiseth to obey his mother, the ravens of the valley shall pick it out, and the young eagles shall eat it (Proverbs 30:17).

Red Horse (Persecution): *"And there went out another horse that, was red: and power was given to him that sat thereon to take peace from the earth, and that they should kill one another: and there was given unto him a great sword (Revelation 6:4)."*

Scorpion (Sin/Evil): *"Behold, I give unto you power to tread on serpents and scorpions, and over all the power of the enemy: and nothing shall by any means hurt you (Luke 10:19)."*

"And thou, son of man, be not afraid of them, neither be afraid of their words, though briers and thorns be with thee, and thou dost dwell among scorpions: be not afraid of their words, nor be dismayed at their looks, though they be a rebellious house (Ezekiel 2:6)."

Serpent (Place your trust in God he is faithful/Satan/Curse/Deceiver): And the Lord said unto Moses, *"Make thee a fiery serpent, and set it upon a pole: and it shall come to pass, that every one that is bitten, when he looketh upon it, shall live (Numbers 21:8)."*

(Satan/Curse): And the Lord God said unto the serpent, *"Because thou hast done this, thou art cursed above all cattle, and above every beast of the field; upon thy belly shalt thou go, and dust shall thou eat all the days of thy life (Genesis 3:14)."*

(Satan the deceiver): But of the fruit of the tree which is in the midst of the garden, God hath said, *"Ye shall not eat of it, neither shall ye touch it, lest ye die."* And the serpent said unto the woman, *"Ye shall not surely die: For God doth know that in the day ye eat thereof, then your eyes shall be opened, and ye shall be as gods, knowing good and evil (Genesis 3:3-5)."*

(Also See Adder/Viper)

Spider/Spider Web (Evil): So are the paths of all that forget God, and the hypocrite's hope shall perish: Whose hope shall be cut off, and whose trust shall be a spider's web. He shall lean upon his house, but it shall not stand: he shall hold it fast, but it shall not endure (Job 8:13-15).

Swine (Deaf and Dumb Spirit): *"Give not that which is holy unto the dogs, neither cast ye your pearls before swine, lest they trample them under their feet, and turn again and rend you (Mathew 7:6)."*

Stork (Birth/Fertility/Springtime): *"Yea, the stork in the heaven knoweth her appointed times; and the turtle and the crane and the swallow observe the time of their coming; but my people know not the judgment of the Lord (Jeremiah 8:7)."*

Vulture (Scavenger): *"There is a path which no fowl knoweth and which the vulture's eye hath not seen (Job 28:7)."*

Whale (Hell): *"For as Jonas was three days and three nights in the whale's belly; so shall the son of man be three days and three nights in the heart of the earth (Mathew 12:40)."*

White Horse (Victory/Purity): *"And I saw heaven opened, and behold a white horse; and he that sat upon him was called Faithful and*

True, and in righteousness he doth judge and make war (Revelation 19:11)."

Wolf (Satan): *"But he that is an hireling, and not the shepherd, whose own the sheep are not, seeth the wolf coming, and leaveth the sheep, and fleeth; and the wolf catcheth them, and scattereth the sheep (John 10:12)."*

"Beware of false prophets, which come to you in sheep's clothing, but inwardly they are ravening wolves (Mathew 7:15)."

CHARACTERS

Angels (Messengers of God): For he shall give his angels charge over thee, to keep thee in all thy ways (Psalm 91:11).

Apostles, The (Jesus named his twelve disciples to the office of apostleship during his ministry here on this Earth/The first officer in the "Five Fold Ministry"): Jesus called his twelve disciples to him and gave them authority to drive out impure spirits and to heal every disease and sickness. These are the names of the twelve apostles: first, Simon (who is called Peter) and his brother Andrew; James son of Zebedee, and his brother John; Philip and Bartholomew; Thomas and Matthew the tax collector; James son of Alphaeus, and Thaddaeus; Simon the Zealot and Judas Iscariot, who betrayed him. These twelve Jesus sent out with the following instructions: *"Do not go among the Gentiles or enter any town of the Samaritans. Go rather to the lost sheep of Israel. As you go, proclaim this message: "The kingdom of heaven has come near (Mathew 10:1-7)."*

Baby (A new believer in Jesus/New ministry/having a Baby): As newborn babes, desire the sincere milk of the word, that ye may grow thereby (1 Peter 2:2).

(New Ministry): *"Before I formed thee in the belly I knew thee; and before thou camest forth out of the womb I sanctified thee, and I ordained thee a prophet unto the nations (Jeremiah 1:5)."*

(Having a Baby): *"Behold, a virgin shall be with child, and shall bring forth a son, and they shall call his name Emmanuel, which being interpreted is, God with us (Mathew 1:23)."*

Baker (Not Listening to God and he withdraws his hand from the people): And he said, *"This will be the manner of the king that shall reign over you: He will take your sons, and appoint them for himself, for his chariots, and to be his horsemen; and some shall run before his chariots. And he will appoint him captains over thousands, and captains over fifties; and will set them to ear his ground, and to reap his harvest, and to make his instruments of war, and instruments of his chariots. And he will take your daughters to be confectionaries, and to be cooks, and to be bakers. And he will take your fields, and your vineyards, and your oliveyards, even the best of them, and give them to his servants (1 Samuel 8:13)."*

Bride (Church/Covenant): And the Spirit and the bride say, *"Come. And let him that heareth say, Come. And let him that is athirst come. And whosoever will, let him take the water of life freely (Revelation 22:17)."*

Bridegroom (Jesus): And while they went to buy, the bridegroom came; and they that were ready went in with him to the marriage: and the door was shut (Mathew 25:10).

Brother (Biological brother or Spiritual brother): Jesus saith unto her, *"Thy brother shall rise again (John 11:23)."*

Carpenter (Christ or to be Christ like to build body of Christ): The carpenter stretcheth out his rule; he marketh it out with a line; he fitteth it with planes, and he marketh it out with the compass, and maketh it after the figure of a man, according to the beauty of a man; that it may remain in the house (Isaiah 44:13).

Children (Children): But when Jesus saw it, he was much displeased, and said unto them, *"Suffer the little children to come unto me, and forbid them not: for of such is the kingdom of God.*

Verily I say unto you, Whosoever shall not receive the kingdom of God as a little child, he shall not enter therein." And he took them up in his arms, put his hands upon them, and blessed them (Mark 10: 14-16).

Clown (Fool): Wherefore he saith, *"Awake thou that sleepest, and arise from the dead, and Christ shall give thee light. See then that ye walk circumspectly, not as fools, but as wise, Redeeming the time, because the days are evil. Wherefore be ye not unwise, but understanding what the will of the Lord is (Ephesians 5:14-17)."*

Daughter (Oneself/Biological daughter): *"Behold, every one that useth proverbs shall use this proverb against thee," saying, "As is the mother, so is her daughter. Thou art thy mother's daughter, that lotheth her husband and her children; and thou art the sister of thy sisters, which lothed their husbands and their children: your mother was an Hittite, and your father an Amorite. And thine elder sister is Samaria, she and her daughters that dwell at thy left hand: and thy younger sister, that dwelleth at thy right hand, is Sodom and her daughters (Ezekiel 16:43-46)."*

Demons/Evil Spirits (Satan's little or big pawns): And in that same hour he cured many of their infirmities and plagues, and of evil spirits; and unto many that were blind he gave sight (Luke 7:21).

FYI: Satan will use "Anything" that will instill fear into you. Most of the time satan will use "Characters" that you have never seen before, however satan will use "Characters" that you have seen before either on television or in a movie for an example. Remember this about Satan: The thief cometh not, but for to steal, and to kill, and to destroy (John 10:10).

Evangelist (A Revivalist/The third officer in the "Five Fold Ministry" according to Ephesians 4:11; And he gave some, apostles; and some, prophets; and some, evangelists; and some, pastors and teachers):

But when they believed Philip preaching the things concerning the kingdom of God, and the name of Jesus Christ, they were baptized, both men and women (Acts 8:12).

Family (Relatives): And the ark of God remained with the family of Obededom in his house three months. And the Lord blessed the house of Obededom, and all that he had (1 Chronicles 13:14).

Farmer (Apostle, Prophet, Evangelist, Pastor & Teacher/Officer of the Five-fold Ministry): *"And these are they which are sown on good ground; such as hear the word, and receive it, and bring forth fruit, some thirtyfold, some sixty, and some an hundred.* And he said unto them, *"Is a candle brought to be put under a bushel, or under a bed? and not to be set on a candlestick? For there is nothing hid, which shall not be manifested; neither was any thing kept secret, but that it should come abroad. If any man have ears to hear, let him hear."* And he said unto them, *"Take heed what ye hear: with what measure ye mete, it shall be measured to you: and unto you that hear shall more be given (Mark 4:20-24)."*

Father (Biological Father and Mother to honor/God/Satan): *"Children, obey your parents in the Lord: for this is right. Honour thy father and mother; which is the first commandment with promise; that it may be well with thee, and thou mayest live long on the earth (Ephesians 6:2)."*

(God): *"Have we not all one father? Hath not one God created us? Why do we deal treacherously every man against his brother, by profaning the covenant of our fathers (Malachi 2:10)?"*

(Satan): Ye are of your father the devil, and the lusts of your father ye will do. He was a murderer from the beginning, and abode not in the truth, because there is no truth in him. When he speaketh a lie, he speaketh of his own: for he is a liar, and the father of it (John 8:44).

Friend (Countenance of friendship): Iron sharpeneth iron; so a man sharpeneth the countenance of his friend (Proverbs 27:17).

Giant (Strongman): *"And there we saw the giants, the sons of Anak, which come of the giants: and we were in our own sight as grasshoppers, and so we were in their sight (Numbers 13:33)."*

God (I am/the Alpha and the Omega/Father): And God said unto Moses, *"I am that I am:"* and he said, *"Thus shalt thou say unto the children of Israel, I am hath sent me unto you"* And God said moreover unto Moses, *"Thus shalt thou say unto the children of Israel, the Lord God of your fathers, the God of Abraham, the God of Isaac, and the God of Jacob, hath sent me unto you: this is my name for ever, and this is my memorial unto all generations (Exodus 3:14-15)."*

(The Alpha and the Omega): And he said unto me, *"It is done. I am Alpha and Omega, the beginning and the end. I will give unto him that is athirst of the fountain of the water of life freely. He that overcometh shall inherit all things; and I will be his God, and he shall be my son. But the fearful, and unbelieving, and the abominable, and murderers, and whoremongers, and sorcerers, and idolaters, and all liars, shall have their part in the lake which burneth with fire and brimstone: which is the second death (Revelation 21:6-8)."*

(Father): Therefore the Jews sought the more to kill him, because he not only had broken the sabbath, but said also that God was his Father, making himself equal with God. Then answered Jesus and said unto them, *"Verily, verily, I say unto you, The Son can do nothing of himself, but what he seeth the Father do: for what things soever he doeth, these also doeth the Son likewise. For the Father loveth the Son, and sheweth him all things that himself doeth: and he will shew him greater works than these, that ye may marvel (John 5:18-20)."*

Groom (Church/Covenant): And the Spirit and the bride say, *"Come. And let him that heareth say, Come. And let him that is athirst come. And whosoever will, let him take the water of life freely (Revelation 22:17)."*

Harlots, Mother of (Seduction): And upon her forehead was a name written, *"Mystery, Babylon the Great, The Mother of Harlots and abominations of the earth (Revelation 17:5)."*

Husband (God has all authority/your husband): For thy Maker is thine husband; the Lord of hosts is his name; and thy Redeemer the Holy One of Israel; The God of the whole earth shall he be called (Isaiah 54:5).

Jesus (The Son of God and The Christ): Therefore the Jews sought the more to kill him, because he not only had broken the sabbath, but said also that God was his Father, making himself equal with God. Then answered Jesus and said unto them, *"Verily, verily, I say unto you, The Son can do nothing of himself, but what he seeth the Father do: for what things soever he doeth, these also doeth the Son likewise. For the Father loveth the Son, and sheweth him all things that himself doeth: and he will shew him greater works than these, that ye may marvel (John 5:18-20)."*

(The Christ): When Jesus came into the coasts of Caesarea Philippi, he asked his disciples, saying, *"Whom do men say that I the Son of man am?"* And they said, *"Some say that thou art John the Baptist: some, Elias; and others, Jeremias, or one of the prophets."* He saith unto them, *"But whom say ye that I am?"* And Simon Peter answered and said, *"Thou art the Christ, the Son of the living God."* And Jesus answered and said unto him, *"Blessed art thou, Simon Barjona: for flesh and blood hath not revealed it unto thee, but my Father which is in heaven. And I say also unto thee, That thou art Peter, and upon this rock I will build my church; and the gates of hell shall not prevail against it. And I will give unto thee the keys of the kingdom of heaven: and whatsoever thou shalt bind on earth shall be bound in heaven: and whatsoever thou shalt loose on earth shall be loosed in heaven."* Then charged he his disciples that they should tell no man that he was Jesus the Christ (Mathew 16:13-20).

(The Saviour): And she brought forth her firstborn son, and wrapped him in swaddling clothes, and laid him in a manger; because there was no room for them in the inn. And there were in the same country shepherds abiding in the field, keeping watch over their flock by night. And, lo, the angel of the Lord came upon them, and the glory of the Lord shone round about them: and they were sore afraid. And the angel said unto them, *"Fear not: for, behold, I bring you good tidings of great joy, which shall be to all people. For unto you is born this day in the city of David a Saviour, which is Christ the Lord. And this shall be a sign unto you; Ye shall find the babe wrapped in swaddling clothes, lying in a manger. And suddenly there was with the angel a multitude of the heavenly host praising God, and saying, Glory to God in the highest, and on earth peace, good will toward men (Luke 2:7-14)."*

Judge (God is our Judge): But the Lord said unto Samuel, *"Look not on his countenance, or on the height of his stature; because I have refused him: for the Lord seeth not as man seeth; for man looketh on the outward appearance, but the Lord looketh on the heart (1 Samuel 16:7)."*

Lawyers (Placed burdens upon men): And he said, *"Woe unto you also, ye lawyers! For ye lade men with burdens grievous to be borne, and ye yourselves touch not the burdens with one of your fingers (Luke 11:46)."*

Man (Angel of the Lord or Evil Spirit): And the angel of the Lord said unto her, *"I will multiply thy seed exceedingly, that it shall not be numbered for multitude (Genesis 16:10)."*

(Evil Spirit): And the evil spirit answered and said, *"Jesus I know, and Paul I know; but who are ye?"* And the man in whom the evil spirit was leaped on them, and overcame them, and prevailed against them, so that they fled out of that house naked and wounded (Acts 19:15-16).

Mother (Eve: "life-giver"/Mother of all living/Biological Mother to honor/Mary is the Mother of Jesus): And Adam called his wife's name Eve; because she was the mother of all living (Genesis 3:20).

(Biological Mother to honor): Children, obey your parents in the Lord: for this is right. Honour thy father and mother; which is the first commandment with promise; That it may be well with thee, and thou mayest live long on the earth (Ephesians 6:2).

(Mary is the Mother of Jesus): And the angel said unto her, *"Fear not, Mary: for thou hast found favour with God. And, behold, thou shalt conceive in thy womb, and bring forth a son, and shalt call his name Jesus. He shall be great, and shall be called the Son of the Highest: and the Lord God shall give unto him the throne of his father David: And he shall reign over the house of Jacob for ever; and of his kingdom there shall be no end."* Then said Mary unto the angel, *"How shall this be, seeing I know not a man?"* And the angel answered and said unto her, *"The Holy Ghost shall come upon thee, and the power of the Highest shall overshadow thee: therefore also that holy thing which shall be born of thee shall be called the Son of God (Luke 2:30-35)."*

(See Harlots, Mother of)

Physician (Jesus is our healer from all sin): When Jesus heard it, he saith unto them, *"They that are whole have no need of the* *physician, but they that are sick: I came not to call the righteous, but sinners to repentance (Mark 2:17)."*

Preacher/Pastor (Good or Evil Messenger/The fourth officer of the "Five Fold Ministry"): (Good messenger): *"And I will give you pastors according to mine heart, which shall feed you with knowledge and understanding (Jeremiah 3:15)."*

(Evil messenger): For such are false apostles, deceitful workers, transforming themselves into the apostles of Christ. And no marvel; for Satan himself is transformed into an angel of light. Therefore it is no great thing if his ministers also be transformed as the ministers of righteousness; whose end shall be according to their works (2 Corinthians 11:13).

Prophet, The (A prophet speaks what God commands to happen in the future/The second officer of the "Five Fold Ministry"): And the Lord said unto Moses, *"See, I have made thee a god to Pharaoh: and Aaron thy brother shall be thy prophet. Thou shalt speak all that I command thee: and Aaron thy brother shall speak unto Pharaoh, that he send the children of Israel out of his land. And I will harden Pharaoh's heart, and multiply my signs and my wonders in the land of Egypt (Exodus 7:1-3)."*

Satan/Lucifer/red dragon/satyr (The rebellious angel who wanted to take God's position and was thrown out of Heaven with a third of the angels that he swayed in this rebellion towards God): *"How art thou fallen from heaven, O Lucifer, son of the morning! How art thou cut down to the ground, which didst weaken the nations (Isaiah 14:12)."*

"And there appeared another wonder in heaven; and behold a great red dragon, having seven heads and ten horns, and seven crowns upon his heads (Revelation 12:3)."

"It shall never be inhabited, neither shall it be dwelt in from generation to generation: neither shall the Arabian pitch tent there; neither shall the shepherds make their fold there. But wild

beasts of the desert shall lie there; and their houses shall be full of doleful creatures; and owls shall dwell there, and satyrs shall dance there. And the wild beasts of the islands shall cry in their desolate houses, and dragons in their pleasant palaces: and her time is near to come, and her days shall not be prolonged (Isaiah 13:20-22)."

Shepherd/Little Bo Peep (Pastor): *"Which may go out before them, and which may go in before them, and which may lead them out, and which may bring them in; that the congregation of the Lord be not as sheep which have no shepherd (Numbers 27:17)."*

Sister (Biological sister/Spiritual sister): *"For whosoever shall do the will of my Father which is in heaven, the same is my brother, and sister, and mother (Mathew 12:50)."*

Soldier (Warfare): *"Thou therefore endure hardness, as a good soldier of Jesus Christ. No man that warreth entangleth himself with the affairs of this life; that he may please him who hath chosen him to be a soldier (2 Timothy 2: 3-4)."*

Son (The Son of God is Jesus/Biological son): *"And we have seen and do testify that the Father sent the Son to be the Saviour of the world. Whosoever shall confess that Jesus is the Son of God, God dwelleth in him, and he in God. And we have known and believed the love that God hath to us. God is love; and he that dwelleth in love dwelleth in God, and God in him (1 John 4:14-16)."*

(Biological son): And he said, *"Take now thy son, thine only son Isaac, whom thou lovest, and get thee into the land of Moriah; and offer him there for a burnt offering upon one of the mountains which I will tell thee of (Genesis 22:2)."*

Teacher (release the word of God/The fifth officer in the "Five Fold Ministry"): The same came to Jesus by night, and said unto him, Rabbi, we know that thou art a teacher come from God: for no man can do these miracles that thou doest, except God be with him. Jesus answered and said unto him, *"Verily,*

verily, I say unto thee, Except a man be born again, he cannot see the kingdom of God (John 3:2-3)."

Thief (Steal and destroy): *"The thief cometh not, but for to steal, and to kill, and to destroy: I am come that they might have life, and that they might have it more abundantly (John 10:10)."*

Wife (Covenant/your wife): *"Therefore shall a man leave his father and his mother, and shall cleave unto his wife: and they shall be one flesh (Genesis 2:24)."*

Witch (Witchcraft): *"For rebellion is as the sin of witchcraft, and stubbornness is as iniquity and idolatry. Because thou hast rejected the word of the Lord, he hath also rejected thee from being king (1 Samuel 15:23)."*

Woman (God's Angels or Evil Spirit): *"Then lifted I up mine eyes, and looked, and, behold, there came out two women, and the wind was in their wings; for they had wings like the wings of a stork: and they lifted up the ephah between the earth and the heaven (Zechariah 5:9)."*

(Evil Spirit): *"Whose ways are crooked, and they froward in their paths: To deliver thee from the strange woman, even from the stranger which flattereth with her words; Which forsaketh the guide of her youth, and forgetteth the covenant of her God (Proverbs 2:16)."*

COLORS

Amber (Fire of God/God's glory): *"Then I beheld, and lo a likeness as the appearance of fire: from the appearance of his loins even downward, fire; and from his loins even upward, as the appearance of brightness, as the colour of amber (Ezekiel 8:2)."*

Black (To have no penitence for sin God will judge those who follow Satan): *"And I beheld when he had opened the sixth seal, and, lo, there was a great earthquake; and the sun became black as sackcloth of hair, and the moon became as blood (Revelation 6:12)."*

Blue (Heaven/The Ten Commandments of God): And upon the table of shewbread they shall spread a cloth of blue, and put thereon the dishes, and the spoons, and the bowls, and covers to cover withal: and the continual bread shall be thereon (Numbers 4:7).

And the Lord spake unto Moses, saying, *"Speak unto the children of Israel, and bid them that they make them fringes in the borders of their garments throughout their generations, and that they put upon the fringe of the borders a ribband of blue: And it shall be unto you for a fringe, that ye may look upon it, and remember all the commandments of the Lord, and do them ; and that ye seek not after your own heart and your own eyes, after which ye use to go a whoring: That ye may remember, and do all my commandments, and be holy unto your God. I am the Lord your God, which brought you out of the land of Egypt, to be your God: I am the Lord your God (Numbers 15:37-41)."*

Brass (God's feet/Trust in God): *"And his feet like unto fine brass, as if they burned in a furnace; and his voice as the sound of many waters (Revelation 1:15)."*

(Trust in God): And the Lord said unto Moses, *"Make thee a fiery serpent, and set it upon a pole: and it shall come to pass, that every one that is bitten, when he looketh upon it, shall live (Numbers 21:8)."*

Brown (No Spirit): *"The grass withereth, the flower fadeth: but the word of our God shall stand for ever (Isaiah 40:8)."*

Gray (Righteousness/The gray area between right and wrong): *"The hoary head is a crown of glory, if it be found in the way of righteousness (Proverbs 16:31)."*

(The gray area between right and wrong): Ephraim, he hath mixed himself among the people; Ephraim is a cake not turned. Strangers have devoured his strength, and he knoweth it not: yea, gray hairs are here and there upon him, yet he knoweth not. And the pride of Israel testifieth to his face: and they do not return to the Lord their God, nor seek him for all this. Ephraim also is like a silly dove without heart: they call to Egypt, they go to Assyria (Hosea 7:8-11).

Green (Prosperity/Life/Envy): And Jacob took him rods of green poplar, and of the hazel and chesnut tree; and pilled white strakes in them, and made the white appear which was in the rods (Genesis 30:37)

(Life): *"And to every beast of the earth, and to every fowl of the air, and to everything that creepeth upon the earth, wherein there is life, I have given every green herb for meat: and it was so (Genesis 1:30)."*

(Envy): *"I have seen the wicked in great power, and spreading himself like a green bay tree (Psalm 37:35)."*

Iron (Strength): *"And the fourth kingdom shall be strong as iron: forasmuch as iron breaketh in pieces and subdueth all things: and as iron that breaketh all these, shall it break in pieces and bruise (Daniel 2:40)."*

Lead (Judgement of God): *"Thou didst blow with thy wind, the sea covered them: they sank as lead in the mighty waters. Who is like unto thee, O Lord, among the gods? Who is like thee, glorious in holiness, fearful in praises, doing wonders? Thou stretchedst out thy right hand, the earth swallowed them (Exodus 15:10-12)."*

Orange (Great Danger/Hell fire is orange): But I say unto you, *"That whosoever is angry with his brother without a cause shall be in danger of the judgment: and whosoever shall say to his brother, Raca, shall be in danger of the council: but whosoever shall say, Thou fool, shall be in danger of hell fire (Mathew 5:22)."*

Pink (Heart of flesh): *"And I will give them one heart, and I will put a new spirit within you; and I will take the stony heart out of their flesh, and will give them an heart of flesh (Ezekiel 11:19)."*

(Stony Heart): *"A sound heart is the life of the flesh: but envy the rottenness of the bones (Proverbs 14:30)."*

Purple (Royalty): Then came Jesus forth, wearing the crown of thorns, and the purple robe. And Pilate saith unto them, *"Behold the man! (John 19:5)."*

Red (The blood of Jesus washes our sins as white as snow/lust/sin/anger/hatred): *"Come now, and let us reason together,"* saith the Lord: *"though your sins be as scarlet, they shall be as white as snow; though they be red like crimson, they shall be as wool (Isaiah 1:18)."*

(lust/sin/anger/hatred): And there went out another horse that was red: and power was given to him that sat thereon to take peace from the earth, and that they should kill one another: and there was given unto him a great sword (Revelation 6:4).

Silver (Knowledge/Wisdom/Prosperity): *"Yea, if thou criest after knowledge, and liftest up thy voice for understanding; If thou seekest her as silver, and searchest for her as for hid treasures (Proverbs 2: 3-4)."*

Tin (Sin): *"And I will turn my hand upon thee, and purely purge away thy dross, and take away all thy tin (Isaiah 1:25)."*

White (Pure/Righteousness): *"And to her was granted that she should be arrayed in fine linen, clean and white: for the fine linen is the righteousness of saints (Revelation 19:8)."*

Yellow or Gold (Wisdom/Glory of God/Prosperity): *"Though ye have lien among the pots, yet shall ye be as the wings of a dove covered with silver, and her feathers with yellow gold (Psalm 68:13)."*

DIRECTIONS

Above (Heaven): Every good gift and every perfect gift is from above, and cometh down from the Father of lights, with whom is no variableness, neither shadow of turning (James 1:17).

Back (Past): But his wife looked back from behind him, and she became a pillar of salt (Genesis 19:26).

Beneath (Hell): Hell from beneath is moved for thee to meet thee at thy coming: it stirreth up the dead for thee, even all the chief ones of the earth; it hath raised up from their thrones all the kings of the nations (Isaiah 14:9).

East (Angel came from the East): And I saw another angel ascending from the east, having the seal of the living God: and he cried with a loud voice to the four angels, to whom it was given to hurt the earth and the sea, saying, *"Hurt not the earth, neither the sea, nor the trees, till we have sealed the servants of our God in their foreheads (Revelation 7:2-3)."*

Front (Future): Write the things which thou hast seen, and the things which are, and the things which shall be hereafter (Revelation 1:19).

Left (Judgement): Then shall he say also unto them on the left hand, *"Depart from me, ye cursed, into everlasting fire, prepared for the devil and his angels: For I was an hungred, and ye gave me no meat: I was thirsty, and ye gave me no drink: I was a stranger, and ye took me not in: naked, and ye clothed me not: sick,* *and in prison, and ye visited me not. Then shall they also answer him, saying, Lord, when saw we thee an hungred, or athirst, or a stranger, or naked, or sick, or in prison, and did not minister unto thee? Then shall he answer them, saying, Verily I say unto you, Inasmuch as ye did it not to one of the least of these, ye did it not to me. And these shall go away into everlasting punishment: but the righteous into life eternal (Mathew 25:41-46)."*

North (Judgement): And the word of the Lord came unto me the second time, saying, *"What seest thou?"* And I said, *"I see a seething pot; and the face thereof is toward the north."* Then the Lord said unto me, *"Out of the north an evil shall break forth upon all the inhabitants of the land. For, lo, I will call all the families of the kingdoms of the north, saith the Lord; and they shall come, and they shall set every one his throne at the entering of the gates of Jerusalem, and against all the walls thereof round about, and against all the cities of Judah. And I will utter my judgments against them touching all their wickedness, who have forsaken me, and have burned incense unto other gods, and worshipped the works of their own hands (Jeremiah 1:13-16)."*

Right (Authority): And Jesus said, *"I am: and ye shall see the Son of man sitting on the right hand of power, and coming in the clouds of heaven (Mark 14:62)."*

South (Judgement): So Joshua smote all the country of the hills, and of the south, and of the vale, and of the springs, and all their kings: he left none remaining, but utterly destroyed all that breathed, as the Lord God of Israel commanded (Joshua 10:40).

West (Judgement): For as the lightning cometh out of the east, and shineth even unto the west; so shall also the coming of the Son of man be (Mathew 24:27).

East, West, North & South (Judgement when Jesus returns to claim his bride): And they shall come from the east, and from the west, and from the north, and from the south, and shall sit down in the kingdom of God (Luke 13:29).

FOOD & DRINK

Apples (Sin): And when the woman saw that the tree was good for food, and that it was pleasant to the eyes, and a tree to be desired to make one wise, she took of the fruit thereof, and did eat, and gave also unto her husband with her; and he did eat (Genesis 3:6).

Bread (Jesus is the bread of life): And Jesus said unto them, *"I am the bread of life: he that cometh to me shall never hunger; and he that believeth on me shall never thirst (John 6:35)."*

Bread flour ("The Wheat" are the Righteous of God): *"Let both grow together until the harvest: and in the time of harvest I will say to the reapers, Gather ye together first the tares, and bind them in bundles to burn them: but gather the wheat into my barn (Mathew 13:30)."*

Butter (Revelation of the Word of God): Butter and honey shall he eat, that he may know to refuse the evil, and choose the good (Isaiah 7:15).

Candy (See Sugar)

Corn (Prosperity): And all countries came into Egypt to Joseph for to buy corn; because that the famine was so sore in all lands (Genesis 41:57).

Grapes (The Fruit of the Righteous/Unrighteous): *"Beware of false prophets, which come to you in sheep's clothing, but inwardly they* *are ravening wolves. Ye shall know them by their fruits. Do men gather grapes of thorns, or figs of thistles? Even so every good tree bringeth forth good fruit; but a corrupt tree bringeth forth evil fruit (Mathew 7:15-17)."*

Honey (Revelation of the Word of God): *"And I took the little book out of the angel's hand, and ate it up; and it was in my mouth sweet as honey: and as soon as I had eaten it, my belly was bitter (Revelation 10:10)."*

Milk (New Christians need the milk first): *"As newborn babes, desire the sincere milk of the word, that ye may grow thereby (1 Peter 2:2)."*

Mozzarella Cheese (Meat): Jesus saith unto them, *"My meat is to do the will of him that sent me, and to finish his work (John 4:34)."*

Oil (The Holy Spirit): *"I have found David my servant; with my holy oil have I anointed him (Psalm 89:20)."*

Salt (To keep the covenant of God or to break God's covenant): For every one shall be salted with fire, and every sacrifice shall be salted with salt. Salt is good: but if the salt have lost his saltness, wherewith will ye season it? Have salt in yourselves, and have peace one with another (Mark 9:49-50).

(To break God's covenant): But his wife looked back from behind him, and she became a pillar of salt (Genesis 19:26).

Sesame Seeds (Manna): Now to Abraham and his seed were the promises made. He saith not, *"And to seeds, as of many; but as of one, and to thy seed, which is Christ (Galatians 3:16)."*

Sugar (Fruit of the Spirit): But the fruit of the Spirit is love, joy, peace, longsuffering, gentleness, goodness, faith, meekness, temperance: against such there is no law. (Galatians 5:22-23).

Water (The Holy Spirit): *"Verily, verily, I say unto thee, Except a man be born of water and of the Spirit, he cannot enter into the kingdom of God. That which is born of the flesh is flesh; and that* which is born of the Spirit is spirit. Marvel not that I said unto thee, Ye must be born again. The wind bloweth where it listeth, and thou hearest the sound thereof, but canst not tell whence it cometh, and whither it goeth: so is every one that is born of the Spirit (John 3:5-8)."

Whole Egg (Ask & you will receive): "If a son shall ask bread of any of you that is a father, will he give him a stone? Or if he ask a fish, will he for a fish give him a serpent? Or if he shall ask an egg, will he offer him a scorpion? If ye then, being evil, know how to give good gifts unto your children: how much more shall your heavenly Father give the Holy Spirit to them that ask him? (Luke 11:11-13)."

Yeast or Leaven (Being Born Again/Repentance): Another parable spake he unto them; "The kingdom of heaven is like unto leaven, which a woman took, and hid in three measures of meal, till the whole was leavened." All these things spake Jesus unto the multitude in parables; and without a parable spake he not unto them: "That it might be fulfilled which was spoken by the prophet, saying, I will open my mouth in parables; I will utter things which have been kept secret from the foundation of the world (Mathew 13:33-36)." The Kingdom spreads like yeast!

NUMBERS

One (Unity/First in rank): In the beginning God created the heaven and the earth. And the earth was without form, and void; and darkness was upon the face of the deep. And the Spirit of God moved upon the face of the waters. And God said, Let there be light: and there was light. And God saw the light, that it was good: and God divided the light from the darkness. And God called the light Day, and the darkness he called Night. And the evening and the morning were the first day (Genesis 1:1-5).

Two (God's judgment/God created heaven on the second day): There went in two and two unto Noah into the ark, the male and the female, as God had commanded Noah. And it came to pass after seven days that the waters of the flood were upon the earth. In the six hundredth year of Noah's life, in the second month, the seventeenth day of the month, the same day were all the fountains of the great deep broken up, and the windows of heaven were opened (Genesis 7:9-11).

(God created heaven on the second day): And God said, *"Let there be a firmament in the midst of the waters, and let it divide the waters from the waters. And God made the firmament, and divided the waters which were under the firmament from the waters which were above the firmament: and it was so. And God called the firmament Heaven. And the evening and the morning were the second day (Genesis 1:6-8)."*

Three (Father, Son & the Holy Spirit): And Jesus came and spake unto them, saying, *"All power is given unto me in heaven and in earth. Go ye therefore, and teach all nations, baptizing them in the name of the Father, and of the Son, and of the Holy Ghost: Teaching them to observe all things whatsoever I have commanded you: and, lo, I am with you always, even unto the end of the world. Amen (Mathew 28:18-20)."*

Four (Harvest of the world): Jesus saith unto them, *"My meat is to do the will of him that sent me, and to finish his work. Say not ye, There are yet four months, and then cometh harvest? behold, I say unto you, Lift up your eyes, and look on the fields; for they are white already to harvest. And he that reapeth receiveth wages, and gathereth fruit unto life eternal: that both he that soweth and he that reapeth may rejoice together. And herein is that saying true, One soweth, and another reapeth. I sent you to reap that whereon ye bestowed no labour: other men laboured, and ye are entered into their labours (John 4:34-38)."*

Five (Government of the five-fold ministry): And he gave some, apostles; and some, prophets; and some, evangelists; and some, pastors and teachers ;(Ephesians 4:11).

Six (God created man on the 6th day): And God said, *"Let us make man in our image, after our likeness: and let them have dominion over the fish of the sea, and over the fowl of the air, and over the cattle, and over all the earth, and over every creeping thing that creepeth upon the earth"* (Genesis 1:26). And God saw everything that he had made, and, behold, it was very good. And the evening and the morning were the sixth day (Genesis 1:31).

Seven (God completed the world & rested/Sanctified/The Seven Spirits of God): And on the seventh day God ended his work which he had made; and he rested on the seventh day from all his work which he had made. And God blessed the seventh day, and sanctified it: because that in it he had rested from all his work which God created and made (Genesis 2:2-3).

(Sanctified): But the seventh day is the sabbath of the Lord thy God: in it thou shalt not do any work, thou, nor thy son, nor thy daughter, thy manservant, nor thy maidservant, nor thy cattle, nor thy stranger that is within thy gates: (Exodus 20:10).

(The Seven Spirits of God): And there shall come forth a rod out of the stem of Jesse, and a Branch shall grow out of his roots: And the spirit of the Lord shall rest upon him, the spirit of wisdom and understanding, the spirit of counsel and might, and the spirit of knowledge and the fear of the Lord. And shall make him of quick understanding in the fear of the Lord: and he shall not judge after the sight of his eyes, neither reprove after the hearing of his ears: but with righteousness shall he judge the poor, and reprove with equity for the meek of the earth: and he shall smite the earth with the rod of his mouth, and with the breath of his lips shall he slay the wicked. And the righteousness shall be the girdle of his loins, and the faithfulness the girdle of his reins (Isaiah 11:1-5). The Seven Spirits of God are Wisdom, Understanding, Counsel, Might, Knowledge, Righteousness and the Fear of the Lord.

Eight (Eighth day Jesus was circumcised/putting off the old man bringing new beginning): And when eight days were accomplished for the circumcising of the child, his name was called Jesus, which was so named of the angel before he was conceived in the womb (Luke 2:21).

In whom also ye are circumcised with the circumcision made without hands, in putting off the body of the sins of the flesh by the circumcision of Christ (Colossians 2:11).

Nine (Judgment of mankind): And about the ninth hour Jesus cried with a loud voice, saying, *"E'-li, E'-li, la'ma sabach'-tha-ni?"* That is to say, *"My God, my God; why hast thou forsaken me (Mathew 27:46)?"* Jesus, when he had cried again with a loud voice, yielded up the ghost. And, behold, the veil of the temple was rent in twain from the top to the bottom; and the earth did quake, and the rocks rent. And the graves were opened: and many bodies of the saints which slept arose, And came out of the graves after his resurrection, and went into the holy city, and appeared unto many. Now when the centurion, and they that were with him, watching Jesus, saw the earthquake, and those things that were done, they feared greatly, saying, *"Truly this was the Son of God (Mathew 27:50-54)."*

FYI: Judgment belongs to God in the *9th* hour showing us that nothing can help us in that hour of darkness once our will is chosen. Jesus knew that it was God's will that he was to sacrifice his life and take on every sin, Jesus also had a will to choose and he chose the will of God. Jesus took on every sin known to mankind. Jesus *yielded up the ghost,* so that we could choose life eternally with him. See how the veil of the temple was broken from the top to the bottom no longer was there anything separating us from God. The earth did quake and the rocks broke and the graves were opened and the saints arose! This proves that Jesus is our redeemer, the saints that were once buried were alive again and they were walking around the holy city, appearing to many! Jesus is the Son of God, just as the fearing centurion said to the Apostle Mathew. Jesus Christ resurrected from the grave just three days after he was crucified, Jesus appeared to many people before his ascension up to heaven. Jesus is the Savior of the world. Jesus is the King of Kings and Lord of Lord, one day every knee will bow and every tongue will confess that Jesus is Lord on that day of

judgment Jesus will judge you depending on how you lived your life here on this earth and for eternity Jesus will either send you to heaven or hell for all of eternity and that my friend is a very, very long time.

Ten (Ten Commandments/God's judgment the ten plagues over Pharaoh the people who followed Pharaoh in Egypt): And he was there with the Lord forty days and forty nights; he did neither eat bread, nor drink water. And he wrote upon the tables the words of the covenant, the Ten Commandments (Exodus 34:28).

(God's judgment the ten plagues over Egypt): **1.) Water to blood:** And the Lord spake unto Moses, Say unto Aaron, *"Take thy rod, and stretch out thine hand upon the waters of Egypt, upon their streams, upon their rivers, and upon their ponds, and upon all their pools of water, that they may become blood; and that there may be blood throughout all the land of Egypt, both in vessels of wood, and in vessels of stone (Exodus 7:19)."* **2.) Frogs:** *"And if thou refuse to let them go, behold, I will smite all thy borders with frogs: And the river shall bring forth frogs abundantly, which shall go up and come into thine house, and into thy bedchamber, and upon thy bed, and into the house of thy servants, and upon thy people, and into thine ovens, and into thy kneadingtroughs: And the frogs shall come up both on thee, and upon thy people, and upon all thy servants (Exodus 8:2-4)."* **3.) Lice:** And the Lord said unto Moses, Say unto Aaron, *"Stretch out thy rod, and smite the dust of the land, that it may become lice throughout all the land of Egypt (Exodus 8:16)."* **4.) Flies:** *"Else, if thou wilt not let my people go, behold, I will send swarms of flies upon thee, and upon thy servants, and upon thy people, and into thy houses: and the houses of the Egyptians shall be full of swarms of flies, and also the ground whereon they are (Exodus 8:21)."* **5.) Livestock Diseased:** *"Behold, the hand of* *the Lord is upon thy cattle which is in the field, upon the horses, upon the asses, upon the camels, upon the oxen, and upon the sheep: there shall be a very grievous murrain (Exodus 9:3)."* **6.) Boils:** And the Lord said unto Moses and unto Aaron, *"Take to you handfuls of ashes of the furnace, and let Moses sprinkle it toward the heaven in the sight of Pharaoh. And it shall become small dust in all the land of Egypt, and shall be a boil breaking forth with blains upon man, and upon beast, throughout all the land of Egypt (Exodus 9:8-9)."* **7.) Thunder and Hail:** And Moses stretched forth his rod toward heaven: and the Lord sent thunder and hail, and the fire ran along upon the ground; and the Lord rained hail upon the land of Egypt (Exodus 9:23). **8.) Locusts:** *"Else, if thou refuse to let my people go, behold, to morrow will I bring the locusts into thy coast: And they shall cover the face of the earth, that one cannot be able to see the earth: and they shall eat the residue of that which is escaped, which remaineth unto you from the hail, and shall eat every tree which groweth for you out of the field (Exodus 10:4-5)."* **9.) Darkness over the land for 3 days:** And the Lord said unto Moses, *"Stretch out thine hand toward heaven, that there may be darkness over the land of Egypt, even darkness which may be felt. And Moses stretched forth his hand toward heaven; and there was a thick darkness in all the land of Egypt three days (Exodus 10:21-22)."* **10.) Death of the firstborn child:** *"And all the firstborn in the land of Egypt shall die, from the first born of Pharaoh that sitteth upon his throne, even unto the firstborn of the maidservant that is behind the mill; and all the firstborn of beasts (Exodus 11:5)."*

Eleven (Prosperity): And about the eleventh hour he went out, and found others standing idle, and saith unto them, *"Why stand ye here all the day idle?"* They say unto him, *"Because no man hath hired us."* He saith unto them, *"Go ye also into the vineyard; and whatsoever is right, that shall ye receive. So when even was come, the* *lord of the vineyard saith unto his steward, Call the labourers, and give them their hire, beginning from the last unto the first."* And when they came that were hired about the eleventh hour, they received every man a penny (Mathew 20:6-9).

Twelve (Joined/government/disciples): *"That ye may eat and drink at my table in my kingdom, and sit on thrones judging the twelve tribes of Israel (Luke 22:30)."*

Now the names of the twelve apostles are these; The first, Simon, who is called Peter, and Andrew his brother; James the son of Zebedee, and John his brother; Philip, and Bartholomew; Thomas, and Matthew the publican; James the son of Alphaeus, and Lebbaeus, whose surname was Thaddaeus; Simon the Canaanite, and Judas Iscariot, who also betrayed him (Mathew 10:2-4).

Fourteen (Passover is celebrated every year as we remember when God delivered the Israelites out of Egypt from slavery): And in the fourteenth day of the first month is the passover of the Lord (Numbers 28:16).

Fifteen (God extends Hezekiah's life 15 years): And I will add unto thy days fifteen years; and I will deliver thee and this city out of the hand of the king of Assyria; and I will defend this city for mine own sake, and for my servant David's sake (2 Kings 20:6).

Sixteen (To rule and reign): Sixteen years old was he when he began to reign, and he reigned two and fifty years in Jerusalem. And his mother's name was Jecholiah of Jerusalem (2 Kings 15:2).

Seventeen (Refuge from the storm): And the ark rested in the seventh month, on the seventeenth day of the month, upon the mountains of Ararat (Genesis 8:4).

Eighteen (Put on Judgment of God/Jesus healed a woman with 18 years of the Spirit of Infirmity): And the anger of the Lord was hot against Israel, and he sold them into the hands of the

Philistines, and into the hands of the children of Ammon. And that year they vexed and oppressed the children of Israel: eighteen years, all the children of Israel that were on the other side Jordan in the land of the Amorites, which is in Gilead (Judges 10: 7-8).

And, behold, there was a woman which had a spirit of infirmity eighteen years, and was bowed together, and could in no wise lift up herself. And when Jesus saw her, he called her to him, and said unto her, *"Woman, thou art loosed from thine infirmity (Luke 13: 11-12)."*

Nineteen (Inheritance): And Iron, and Migdalel, Horem, and Bethanath, and Bethshemesh; nineteen cities with their villages. This is the inheritance of the tribe of the children of Naphtali according to their families, the cities and their villages. (Joshua 19: 38-39).

Twenty (Measurement): And the oracle in the forepart was twenty cubits in length, and twenty cubits in breadth, and twenty cubits in the height thereof: and he overlaid it with pure gold; and so covered the altar which was of cedar (1 Kings 6:20).

Forty (God's Judgment): *"For yet seven days, and I will cause it to rain upon the earth forty days and forty nights; and every living substance that I have made will I destroy from off the face of the earth (Genesis 7:4)."*

Fifty (The *Holy Ghost* came *50* days after the *Passover* on the *50th* day which is called the day of Pentecost and is celebrated because *the church* this is a *turning point for the church.* The *Holy Ghost* filled them and they began to speak in other tongues.): And when the day of Pentecost was fully come, they were all with one accord in one place. And suddenly there came a sound from heaven as of a rushing mighty wind, and it filled all the house where they were sitting. And there appeared unto them cloven tongues like as of fire, and it sat upon each of them. And they were all filled with the Holy Ghost, and began to speak with other tongues, as the Spirit gave them utterance (Acts 2:1-4).

Hundred (Isaac is the *promise* that God gave Abraham he would have a son, even though Abraham was a hundred years old when Isaac was born, always know that God will fulfill his *promises*): And Abraham was an hundred years old, when his son Isaac was born unto him (Genesis 21:5).

(Isaac received a *hundredfold* he is the *promise (generation)*, that God *promised* Abraham because Abraham showed God that he would have sacrificed his only son *Isaac* to God, then God said that his seed would receive the *promise* that he would *bless* his generation.): Then Isaac sowed in that land, and received in the same year an hundredfold: and the Lord blessed him (Genesis 26:12). And the Lord appeared unto him the same night, and said, *"I am the God of Abraham thy father: fear not, for I am with thee, and will bless thee, and multiply thy seed for my servant Abraham's sake (Genesis 26:24)."*

Six, six, six (666) (The mark of the beast): And he had power to give life unto the image of the beast, that the image of the beast should both speak, and cause that as many as would not worship the image of the beast should be killed. And he causeth all, to be killed. And he causeth all, both small and great, rich and poor, free and bond, to receive a mark in their right hand, or in their foreheads. And that no man might buy or sell, save he that had the mark, or the name of the beast, or the number of his name. Here is wisdom. Let him that hath understanding count the number of the beast: for it is the number of a man; and his number is Six hundred threescore and six (Revelation 13.15-18).

Thousand (Prosperity): And unto Sarah he said, *"Behold, I have given thy brother a thousand pieces of silver: behold, he is to thee a covering of the eyes, unto all that are with thee, and with all other: thus she was reproved (Genesis 20:16)."*

MISCELLANEOUS

Airplane (Travel/Ministry): And he rode upon a cherub, and did fly: yea, he did fly upon the wings of the wind (Psalm 18:10).

(Ministry): And he made him to ride in the second chariot which he had; and they cried before him, Bow the knee: and he made him ruler over all the land of Egypt (Genesis 41:43).

Adultery (Sin): But I say unto you, *"That whosoever looketh on a woman to lust after her hath committed adultery with her already in his heart (Mathew 5:28)."*

Anchor (Steadfast): That by two immutable things, in which it was impossible for God to lie, we might have a strong consolation, who have fled for refuge to lay hold upon the hope set before us: Which hope we have as an anchor of the soul, both sure and stedfast, and which entereth into that within the veil (Hebrews 6:18-19).

Ankles (Weak): And when the man that had the line in his hand went forth eastward, he measured a thousand cubits, and he brought me through the waters; the waters were to the ankles (Ezekiel 47:3).

Ark of the Testimony (God rested in this place): *"And thou shalt put the mercy seat above upon the ark; and in the ark thou shalt put the testimony that I shall give thee. And there I will meet with thee, and I will commune with thee from above the mercy seat, from between the two cherubims which are upon the ark of* *the testimony, of all things which I will give thee in command-ment unto the children of Israel (Exodus 25:21-22)."*

Arm (God's Strength): *"With a strong hand, and with a stretched out arm: for his mercy endureth for ever. To him which divided the Red sea into parts: for his mercy endureth for ever: And made Israel to pass through the midst of it: for his mercy endureth for ever (Psalm 136:12)."*

Armour of God (Spiritual Armour for Warfare): *"Wherefore take unto you the whole armour of God that ye may be able to withstand in the evil day, and having done all, to stand (Ephesians 6:13)."*

Arrows (Gossip): *"Who whet their tongue like a sword, and bend their bows to shoot their arrows, even bitter words (Psalm 64:3)."*

Ashes (Repentance): *"Hear, I beseech thee, and I will speak: I will demand of thee, and declare thou unto me. I have heard of thee by the hearing of the ear: but now mine eye seeth thee. Wherefore I abhor myself, and repent in dust and ashes (Job 42:4-6)."*

Atom Bombs (War between the Nations): *"For nation shall rise against nation, and kingdom against kingdom: and there shall be earthquakes in divers places, and there shall be famines and trou-bles: these are the beginnings of sorrows (Mark 13:8)."*

Attic (Put off memories of the past that hinder you): *"Wherefore henceforth know we no man after the flesh: yea, though we have known Christ after the flesh, yet now henceforth know we him no more. Therefore if any man be in Christ, he is a new creature: old things are passed away; behold, all things are become new. And all things are of God, who hath reconciled us to himself by Jesus Christ, and hath given to us the ministry of reconciliation (2 Corinthians 5:16-18)."*

Autumn Leaves (Repentance): *"Thou meetest him that rejoiceth and worketh righteousness, those that remember thee in thy ways: behold, thou art wroth; for we have sinned: in those is continu-*

ance, and we shall be saved. But we are all as an unclean thing, and all our righteousnesses are as filthy rags; and we all do fade as a leaf; and our iniquities, like the wind, have taken us away (Isaiah 64:5-6)." **(Also See; Leaves, Green).**

Axe (Word/Gospel): *"And now also the axe is laid unto the root of the trees: therefore every tree which bringeth not forth good fruit is hewn down, and cast into the fire (Mathew 3:10)."*

Back (See in Chapter on Directions)

Balance (s) (God's Judgement): And when he had opened the third seal, I heard the third beast say, Come and see. And I beheld, and lo a black horse; and he that sat on him had a pair of balances in his hand. And I heard a voice in the midst of the four beasts say, A measure of wheat for a penny, and three measures of barley for a penny; and see thou hurt not the oil and the wine (Revelation 6:5-6).

Bank (Heaven): *"But lay up for yourselves treasures in heaven, where neither moth nor rust doth corrupt, and where thieves do not break through nor steal (Mathew 6:20)."*

Banners (See Flag)

Barn (Storehouse to hold your blessings): *"Honour the Lord with thy substance, and with the firstfruits of all thine increase: So shall thy barns be filled with plenty, and thy presses shall burst out with new wine (Proverbs 3:9-10)."*

Bathing (Sanctification by the word of God): *" Husbands, love your wives, even as Christ also loved the church, and gave himself for it; That he might sanctify and cleanse it with the washing of water by the word (Ephesians 5:25-26)."*

Bathroom (To use the bathroom (repentance) or not the use the bathroom (hold onto sin): Wash you, make you clean; put away the evil of your doings from before mine eyes; cease to do evil (Isaiah 1:16).

Bed (Covenant/broken covenant): *"Marriage is honourable in all, and the bed undefiled: but whoremongers and adulterers God will judge (Hebrews 13:4)."*

Bicycle (Children's Ministry): *"If ye then, being evil, know how to give good gifts unto your children, how much more shall your Father which is in heaven give good things to them that ask him (Mathew 7:11)?"*

Binoculars (Insight from the Holy Spirit): *"Howbeit when he, the Spirit of truth, is come, he will guide you into all truth: for he shall not speak of himself; but whatsoever he shall hear, that shall he speak: and he will shew you things to come (John 16:13)."*

Bleeding (Persecution): *"Blessed are they which are persecuted for righteousness' sake: for theirs is the kingdom of heaven (Mathew 5:10)."*

Blind (Ignorant): *"Let them alone: they be blind leaders of the blind. And if the blind lead the blind, both shall fall into the ditch (Mathew 15:14)."*

Blood (Blood of Jesus purifies all sin): *"And from Jesus Christ, who is the faithful witness, and the first begotten of the dead, and the prince of the kings of the earth. Unto him that loved us, and washed us from our sins in his own blood (Revelation 1:5)."*

Boat/Ship/Shipwreck (Personal ministry/Shipwreck/lacking faith in God): A window shalt thou make to the ark, and in a cubit shalt thou finish it above; and the door of the ark shalt thou set in the side thereof; with lower, second, and third stories shalt thou make it (Genesis 6:16).

(Shipwreck, lacking faith in God): *"Holding faith, and a good conscience; which some having put away concerning faith have made shipwreck (1 Timothy 1:19)."*

Books (Gods Knowledge): *"Ye are our epistle written in our hearts, known and read of all men (2 Corinthians 3:2)."* **(See Lambs book of life)**

Bones that were dead, seeing the slain brought back to life from God, the coming together of (To prophesy according to the will of the Lord, and those who were dead are given life again, God is our creator he can do anything): So I prophesied as I was commanded: and as I prophesied, there was a noise, and behold a shaking, and the flesh came upon them, and the skin covered them above: but there was no breath in them. Then said he unto me, *"Prophesy unto the wind, prophesy, son of man, and say to the wind,* Thus saith the Lord God; *Come from the four winds, O breath, and breathe upon these slain, that thy may live."* So I prophesied as he commanded me, and the breath came into them, and they lived, and stood upon their feet, an exceeding great army (Ezekiel 37:7-10).

Brakes, No (Hindrance): *"Having eyes full of adultery, and that cannot cease from sin; beguiling unstable souls: an heart they have exercised with covetous practices; cursed children (2 Peter 2:14)."*

Branches/Vine (Saints "Abiding" in God bring forth fruit): *"I am the vine, ye are the branches: He that abideth in me, and I in him, the same bringeth forth much fruit: for without me ye can do nothing (John 15:5)."*

Brazen Altar (to sacrifice): *"And he shall put his hand upon the head of the burnt offering; and it shall be accepted for him to make atonement for him (Leviticus 1:4)."*

Bride Dress (Righteousness): *"And to her was granted that she should be arrayed in fine linen, clean and white: for the fine linen is the righteousness of saints (Revelation 19:8)."*

Bridge (Faith): *"There hath no temptation taken you but such as is common to man: but God is faithful, who will not suffer you to be tempted above that ye are able; but will with the temptation also make a way to escape, that ye may be able to bear it (1 Corinthians 10:13)."*

Calendar (Covenant/Time): *"But my covenant will I establish with Isaac, which Sarah shall bear unto thee at this set time in the next year (Genesis 17:21)."*

Candlestick (The Church): *"The mystery of the seven stars which thou sawest in my right hand, and the seven golden candlesticks. The seven stars are the angels of the seven churches: and the seven candlesticks which thou sawest are the seven churches (Revelation 1:20)."*

Car (Ministry): *"And he made him to ride in the second chariot which he had; and they cried before him, Bow the knee: and he made him ruler over all the land of Egypt (Genesis 41:43)."* God will use your personal vehicle to show you your ministry.

Cave (People hiding from the judgement of God): *"And they shall go into the holes of the rocks, and into the caves of the earth, for fear of the Lord, and for the glory of his majesty, when he ariseth to shake terribly the earth (Isaiah 2:19)."*

Censer (A container you place incense in): *"And another angel came and stood at the altar, having a golden censer; and there was given unto him much incense, that he should offer it with the prayers of all saints upon the golden altar which was before the throne (Revelation 8:3)."*

Chain (Bondage to sin): *"For he had commanded the unclean spirit to come out of the man. For oftentimes it had caught him: and he was kept bound with chains and in fetters; and he brake the bands, and was driven of the devil into the wilderness (Luke 8:29)."*

Chair (Position of Authority): *"And love the uppermost rooms at feasts, and the chief seats in the synagogues (Mathew 23:6)."*

Chariot (New Ministry): And Pharaoh took off his ring from his hand, and put it upon Joseph's hand, and arrayed him in vestures of fine linen, and put a gold chain about his neck; And he made him to ride in the second chariot which he had; and they cried before him, *"Bow the knee:"* and he made him ruler over all the land of Egypt. (Genesis 41:42-43).

Choked, being (To hinder/to kill): *"And the cares of this world, and the deceitfulness of riches, and the lusts of other things entering in, choke the word, and it becometh unfruitful (Mark 4:19)."*

Church (To keep the Sabbath day holy which is the Fourth commandment of the Ten Commandments given to Moses by God): *"Ye shall keep the sabbath therefore; for it is holy unto you: every one that defileth it shall surely be put to death: for whosoever doeth any work therein, that soul shall be cut off from among his people. Six days may work be done; but in the seventh is the sabbath of rest, holy to the Lord: whosoever doeth any work in the sabbath day, he shall surely be put to death. Wherefore the children of Israel shall keep the sabbath, to observe the sabbath throughout their generations, for a perpetual covenant (Exodus 31:14-16)."*

Circle (Decree with a ring): *"Write ye also for the Jews, as it liketh you, in the king's name, and seal it with the king's ring: for the writing which is written in the king's name, and sealed with the king's ring, may no man reverse (Esther 8:8)."*

City (The Church): *"Ye are the light of the world. A city that is set on an hill cannot be hid (Mathew 5:14)."*

Cliff, falling off a (Losing your salvation): *"Thy vows are upon me, O God: I will render praises unto thee. For thou hast delivered my soul from death: wilt not thou deliver my feet from falling, that I may walk before God in the light of the living (Psalm 56:12-13)?"*

Clock (Time): *"Redeeming the time, because the days are evil (Ephesians 5:16)."*

Closet (Private): *"But thou, when thou prayest, enter into thy closet, and when thou hast shut thy door, pray to thy Father which is in secret; and thy Father which seeth in secret shall reward thee openly (Mathew 6:6)."*

Clothing (Clean Righteousness/Dirty Clothes Unrighteousness) *"But put ye on the Lord Jesus Christ, and make not provision for the flesh, to fulfill the lusts thereof (Romans 13:14)."*

(Dirty Clothes Unrighteousness): *"For if there come unto your assembly a man with a gold ring, in goodly apparel, and there come in also a poor man in vile raiment (James 2:2)."*

Coal being placed upon your lips or someone else's lips (Cleanse your lips from sin): *"Then said I, Woe is me! For I am undone; because I am a man of unclean lips, and I dwell in the midst of a people of unclean lips: for mine eyes have seen the King, the Lord of hosts. Then flew one of the seraphims unto me, having a live coal in his hand, which he had taken with the tongs from off the altar: And he laid it upon my mouth, and said, Lo, this hath touched thy lips; and thine iniquity is taken away, and thy sin purged (Isaiah 6:5-7)."*

Comforter, new comforter in a bag being placed upon a shelf) (One that has been *Born of the Spirit* and places the *Holy Spirit* in a bag to *quench* the *Holy Spirit*; a/k/a *The Comforter*): *"In everything give thanks: for this is the will of God in Christ Jesus concerning you. Quench not the Spirit. Despise not prophesyings. Prove all things; hold fast that which is good. Abstain from all appearance of evil (1 Thessalonians 5:18-22)."*

Couch (Rest): That lie upon beds of ivory, and stretch themselves upon their couches, and eat the lambs out of the flock, and the calves out of the midst of the stall (Amos 6:4).

Cloud & Fiery Pillar (God's guidance): And the Lord went before them by day in a pillar of a cloud, to lead them the way; and by night in a pillar of fire, to give them light; to go by day and night (Exodus 13:21).

Cloud of Witness, the Great (Saints in heaven/family/friends that are in heaven watching you on this Earth seeing what you are doing for God): *"Wherefore seeing we also are com-*

passed about with so great a cloud of witnesses, let us lay aside every weight, and the sin which doth so easily beset us, and let us run with patience the race that is set before us (Hebrews 12:1)."

Cross (Jesus willingly gave his life for the remission of all sin then arose on the third day defeating death so that we can willingly choose to live eternally in Heaven with him): *"And he bearing his cross went forth into a place called the place of a skull, which is called in the Hebrew Golgotha: Where they crucified him, and two other with him, on either side one, and Jesus in the midst (John 19:17-18)."*

Crown (Crown of righteousness given by the Lord when we enter into eternity in Heaven for fighting the good fight of faith): *"I have fought a good fight, I have finished my course, I have kept the faith: Henceforth there is laid up for me a crown of righteousness, which the Lord, the righteous judge, shall give me at that day: and not to me only, but unto all them also that love his appearing. Do thy diligence to come shortly unto me (2 Timothy 4:7-9)."*

Crown of Thorns: (Thorns represent sin/Jesus took on every sin known and broke the curse that God spoke against humanity when he wore the "Crown of Thorns "and was crucified): And unto Adam he said, *"Because thou hast hearkened unto the voice of thy wife, and hast eaten of the tree, of which I commanded thee, saying, Thou shalt not eat of it: cursed is the ground for thy sake; in sorrow shalt thou eat of it all the days of thy life; Thorns also and thistles shall it bring forth to thee; and thou shalt eat the herb of the field (Genesis 3:17-18)."*

Cup (Good/Evil/Cup of iniquity): And Joseph said unto them, *"What deed is this that ye have done? wot ye not that such a man as I can certainly divine?"* And Judah said, *"What shall we say unto my lord? what shall we speak? or how shall we clear ourselves? God hath found out the iniquity of thy servants: behold, we are my lord's servants, both we, and he also with whom the* *cup is found."* And he said, *"God forbid that I should do so: but the man in whose hand the cup is found, he shall be my servant; and as for you, get you up in peace unto your father (Genesis 44:15)."*

"For her sins have reached unto heaven, and God hath remembered her iniquities. Reward her even as she rewarded you, and double unto her double according to her works: in the cup which she hath filled fill to her double. How much she hath glorified herself, and lived deliciously, so much torment and sorrow give her: for she saith in her heart, I sit a queen, and am no widow, and shall see no sorrow (Revelation 18:5-7)."

Dancing (Worship): *"And David danced before the Lord with all his might; and David was girded with a linen ephod (2 Samuel 6:14)."*

Darkness (Night/Gods Judgment/Wickedness): *"And God called the light Day, and the darkness he called Night. And the evening and the morning were the first day (Genesis 1:5)."*

(God's Judgment): And the Lord said unto Moses, *"Stretch out thine hand toward heaven, that there may be darkness over the land of Egypt, even darkness which may be felt. And Moses stretched forth his hand toward heaven; and there was a thick darkness in all the land of Egypt three days (Exodus 10:21-22)."*

(Wickedness): *"For we wrestle not against flesh and blood, but against principalities, against powers, against the rulers of the darkness of this world, against spiritual wickedness in high places (Ephesians 6:12)."*

Day (God called the Light "Day"): *"And God called the light Day, and the darkness he called Night. And the evening and the morning were the first day (Genesis 1:5)."*

Desert (Wilderness/Lost souls): The voice that cryeth out in the wilderness, *"Prepare ye the way of the Lord, make straight in the desert a highway for our God (Isaiah 40:3)."*

Die, to (To die to your flesh and become a new person walking in the righteousness of God): That ye put off concerning the former conversation the old man, which is corrupt according to the deceitful lusts; And be renewed in the spirit of your mind; And that ye put on the new man, which after God is created in righteousness and true holiness (Ephesians 4:22-24).

Ditch (See Pit)

Dominoes (Chastisement from God for disobedience): *"And they shall fall one upon another, as it were before a sword, when none pursueth: and ye shall have no power to stand before your enemies (Leviticus 26:37)."*

Door (Blessings from God for obedience): *"I know thy works: behold, I have set before thee an open door, and no man can shut it: for thou hast a little strength, and hast kept my word, and hast not denied my name (Revelation 3:8)."*

Drowning (Unrighteousness): *"Because thou hast forgotten the God of thy salvation, and hast not been mindful of the rock of thy strength, therefore shalt thou plant pleasant plants, and shalt set it with strange slips: In the day shalt thou make thy plant to grow, and in the morning shalt thou make thy seed to flourish: but the harvest shall be a heap in the day of grief and of desperate sorrow. Woe to the multitude of many people, which make a noise like the noise of the seas; and to the rushing of nations, that make a rushing like the rushing of mighty waters (Isaiah 17:10-12)."*

Drycleaner (Repentance): And God said unto Jacob, *"Arise, go up to Bethel, and dwell there: and make there an altar unto God, that appeared unto thee when thou fleddest from the face of Esau thy brother."* Then Jacob said unto his household, and to all that were with him, *"Put away the strange gods that are among you, and be clean, and change your garments: And let us arise, and go up to Bethel; and I will make there an altar unto God, who* answered me in the day of my distress, and was with me in the way which I went (Genesis 35:1-3)."

Dust (Man/Woman): "And the Lord God formed man of the dust of the ground, and breathed into his nostrils the breath of life; and man became a living soul (Genesis 2:7)."

Ears (To Hear God): "He that hath ears to hear, let him hear (Mathew 11:15)."

Earthquakes (A sign of the times before Jesus returns): "For nation shall rise against nation, and kingdom against kingdom: and there shall be famines, and pestilences, and earthquakes, in divers places (Mathew 24:7)."

Eyes (Foresight from God/Represents the light (righteousness) or darkness (unrighteousness) in the body): "But blessed are your eyes, for they see: and your ears, for they hear (Mathew 13:16)."

Represents the light (righteousness) or darkness (unrighteousness) in the body: "The light of the body is the eye: therefore when thine eye is single, thy whole body also is full of light; but when thine eye is evil, thy body also is full of darkness (Luke 11:34)."

Falling (See falling off a Cliff)

Feathers (Presence of the Lord and his angels): "He that dwelleth in the secret place of the most High shall abide under the shadow of the Almighty (Psalm 91:1)."

Feet (To prepare to preach the gospel): "And your feet shod with the preparation of the gospel of peace (Ephesians 6:15)."

Fence (Religious barrier): "And I will make thee unto this people a fenced brasen wall: and they shall fight against thee, but they shall not prevail against thee: for I am with thee to save thee and to deliver thee, saith the Lord (Jeremiah 15:20)."

Finger (Discernment): This they said, tempting him that they might have to accuse him. But Jesus stooped down, and with his finger wrote on the ground, as though he heard them not. So when they continued asking him, he lifted up himself, and said unto them, *"He that is without sin among you, let him first cast a stone at her (John 8:6-7)."*

Fire (God's Word): *"Is not my word like as a fire? saith the Lord; and like a hammer that breaketh the rock in pieces (Jeremiah 23:29)?"*

Flag or Banner (Declaring that God hears and answers our petitions to him; denoting Standards, Victory through battle, Identification that we belong to God, and Praise):

(Standards): *"We will rejoice in thy salvation, and in the name of our God we will set up our banners: the Lord fulfill all thy petitions. Now know I that the Lord saveth his anointed; he will hear him from his holy heaven with the saving strength of his right hand. Some trust in chariots, and some in horses: but we will remember the name of the Lord our God. They are brought down and fallen: but we are risen, and stand upright. Save, Lord: let the king hear us when we call (Psalm 20:5-9)."*

(Victory through battle; "Jehovahnissi" means "The Lord is my Banner"): And Joshua discomfited Amalek and his people with the edge of the sword. And the Lord said unto Moses, *"Write this for a memorial in a book, and rehearse it in the ears of Joshua: for I will utterly put out the remembrance of Amalek from under heaven."* And Moses built an altar, and called the name of it Jehovahnissi: For he said, *"Because the Lord hath sworn that the Lord will have war with Amalek from generation to generation (Exodus 17:13-16)."*

(Identification that we belong to God): And the Lord spake unto Moses and unto Aaron, saying, *"Every man of the children of Israel shall pitch by his own standard, with the ensign of their father's house: far off about the tabernacle of the congregation shall they pitch, and on the east side toward the rising of the sun shall they of the standard of the camp of Judah pitch throughout their armies: and Nahshon the son of Amminadab shall be captain of the children of Judah (Numbers 2:1-3)."*

(Praise*): "We will rejoice in thy salvation, and in the name of our God we will set up our banners: the Lord fulfill all thy petitions. Now know I that the Lord saveth his anointed; he will hear him from his holy heaven with the saving strength of his right hand. Some trust in chariots, and some in horses: but we will remember the name of the Lord our God. They are brought down and fallen: but we are risen, and stand upright. Save, Lord: let the king hear us when we call (Psalm 20:5-9)."*

Footstool (Victory): The Lord said unto my Lord, *"Sit thou at my right hand, until I make thine enemies thy footstool (Psalm 110:1)."*

Forest (Nations): *"I have blotted out, as a thick cloud, thy transgressions, and, as a cloud, thy sins: return unto me; for I have redeemed thee. Sing, O ye heavens; for the Lord hath done it: shout, ye lower parts of the earth: break forth into singing, ye mountains, O forest, and every tree therein: for the Lord hath redeemed Jacob, and glorified himself in Israel (Isaiah 44:22-23)."*

Fortress (God's protection): And he said, *"The Lord is my rock, and my fortress, and my deliverer (2 Samuel 22:2)."*

Gloves (Covering): *"Who shall ascend into the hill of the Lord? Or who shall stand in his holy place? He that hath clean hands, and a pure heart; who hath not lifted up his soul unto vanity, nor sworn deceitfully (Psalm 24:3-4)."*

"The Golden Gate Bridge" a/k/a The Eastern Gate in Jerusalem (King Jesus will return through the Eastern Gate): Then he brought me back the way of the gate of the outward sanctuary which looketh toward the east; and it was shut. Then said the Lord unto me; *"This gate shall be shut, it shall not be opened, and no man shall enter in by it; because the Lord, the God of Israel, hath entered in by it, therefore it shall be shut. It is for* *the prince; the prince, he shall sit in it to eat bread before the Lord; he shall enter by the way of the porch of that gate, and shall go out by the way of the same (Ezekiel 44:1-3)."*

FYI: God showed me in a dream the "Golden Gate Bridge" in California. The "Golden Gate Bridge" is also called "The Eastern Gate." In this dream God showed me the "Golden Gate Bridge" as a representation only of "The Eastern Gate" that is in Jerusalem.

Graveyard/graves (Hypocrites): Woe unto you, scribes and Pharisees, hypocrites! For ye are as graves which appear not, and the men that walk over them are not aware of them (Luke 11:44).

Green Pastures/Mowed Grass (Restoration): *"The Lord is my shepherd; I shall not want. He maketh me to lie down in green pastures: he leadeth me beside the still waters. He restoreth my soul: he leadeth me in the paths of righteousness for his name's sake. Yea, though I walk through the valley of the shadow of death, I will fear no evil: for thou art with me; thy rod and thy staff they comfort me. Thou preparest a table before me in the presence of mine enemies: thou anointest my head with oil; my cup runneth over. Surely goodness and mercy shall follow me all the days of my life: and I will dwell in the house of the Lord for ever (Psalm 23)."*

Guns/Bullets (Gossip/Without ability or authority): *"Who whet their tongue like a sword, and bend their bows to shoot their arrows, even bitter words: That they may shoot in secret at the perfect: suddenly do they shoot at him, and fear not (Psalm 64:3-4)?"*

(Without ability or authority): *"When a strongman keepeth his peace, his goods are in peace: But when a stronger than he shall come upon him, and overcome him, he taketh from him all his armour wherein he trusted, and divideth his spoils. He that is not with me is against me: and he that gathereth not with me scattereth (Luke 11:21-23).*

Hail (Judgment): *"I smote you with blasting and with mildew and with hail in all the labours of your hands; yet ye turned not to me,"* saith the Lord (Haggai 2:17).

Hair (Covering/strength): That he told her all his heart, and said unto her, *"There hath not come a razor upon mine head; for I have been a Nazarite unto God from my mother's womb: if I be shaven, then my strength will go from me, and I shall become weak, and be like any other man (Judges 16:17)."*

Hammer (Word of God): *"Is not my word like as a fire?"* saith the Lord; *"and like a hammer that breaketh the rock in pieces (Jeremiah 23:29)?"*

Hands (Works/Good or Evil): *"For thou shalt eat the labour of thine hands: happy shalt thou be, and it shall be well with thee (Psalm 128:2)."*

"Give them according to their deeds, and according to the wickedness of their endeavours: give them after the work of their hands; render to them their desert (Psalm 28:4)."

Harp (Sing unto the Lord): *"Make a joyful noise unto the Lord, all the earth: make a loud noise, and rejoice, and sing praise. Sing unto the Lord with the harp; with the harp, and the voice of a psalm. With trumpets and sound of cornet make a joyful noise before the Lord, the King (Psalm 98:4-6)."*

Hat/Helmet (Covering): *"For he put on righteousness as a breastplate, and an helmet of salvation upon his head; and he put on the garments of vengeance for clothing, and was clad with zeal as a cloak (Isaiah 59:17)."*

Head (Authority): *"But I would have you know, that the head of every man is Christ; and the head of the woman is the man; and the head of Christ is God (1 Corinthians 11:3)."*

Heart (Good or Evil): *"A good man out of the good treasure of his heart bringeth forth that which is good; and an evil man out of the evil treasure of his heart bringeth forth that which is evil: for of the abundance of the heart his mouth speaketh (Luke 6:45)."*

Helicopter (Hovering): *"Be still, and know that I am God. I will be exalted among the heathen, I will be exalted in the earth (Psalm 46:10)."*

Hills (God's Judgement/Trials/Generational Blessings): *"And the waters prevailed, and were increased greatly upon the earth; and the ark went upon the face of the waters. And the waters prevailed exceedingly upon the earth; and all the high hills that were under the whole heaven were covered. Fifteen cubits upward did the waters prevail; and the mountains were covered (Genesis 7:18-20)."*

(Trials): *"I will lift up mine eyes unto the hills, from whence cometh my help. My help cometh from the Lord, which made heaven and earth. He will not suffer thy foot to be moved: he that keepeth thee will not slumber (Psalm 121:1-3)."*

(Generational Blessings): *"The blessings of thy father have prevailed above the blessings of my progenitors unto the utmost bound of the everlasting hills: they shall be on the head of Joseph, and on the crown of the head of him that was separate from his brethren (Genesis 49:26)."*

Highway/Path (Righteousness/Unrighteousness): *"And an highway shall be there, and a way, and it shall be called The way of holiness; the unclean shall not pass over it; but it shall be for those: the wayfaring men, though fools, shall not err therein (Isaiah 35:8)."*

(Unrighteousness): Thus saith the Lord, *"Stand ye in the ways, and see, and ask for the old paths, where is the good way, and walk therein, and ye shall find rest for your souls."* But they said, *"We will not walk therein (Jeremiah 6:16)."*

Homosexual Acts (Abomination): *"Thou shalt not lie with mankind, as with womankind: it is abomination (Leviticus 18:22)."*

Horns (Authority): *"And it shall come to pass, that when they make a long blast with the ram's horn, and when ye hear the sound of the trumpet, all the people shall shout with a great shout; and the wall of the city shall fall down flat, and the people shall ascend up every man straight before him (Joshua 6:5)."*

FYI: Oil was carried in the horn and used to sanctify before a sacrifice to the Lord: And the Lord said to Samuel, *"How long wilt thou mourn for Saul, seeing I have rejected him from reigning over Israel? Fill thine horn with oil, and go, I will send thee to Jesse the Bethlehemite: for I have provided me a king among his sons."* **And Samuel said,** *"How can I go? If Saul hear it, he will kill me."* **And the Lord said,** *"Take an heifer with thee, and say, I am come to sacrifice to the Lord. And call Jesse to the sacrifice, and I will shew thee what thou shalt do: and thou shalt anoint unto me him whom I name unto thee."* **And Samuel did that which the Lord spake, and came to Bethlehem. And the elders of the town trembles at his coming, and said,** *"Comest thou peaceably?"* **And he said,** *"Peaceably, I am come to sacrifice unto the Lord: sanctify yourselves, and come with me to the sacrifice."* **And he sanctified Jesse and his sons, and called them to the sacrifice (1 Samuel 16:1-5).**

Hotel/Inn (Church): And she brought forth her firstborn son, and wrapped him in swaddling clothes, and laid him in a manger; because there was no room for them in the inn (Luke 2:7).

House/Old House (You personally): *"For we know that if our earthly house of this tabernacle were dissolved, we have a building of God, an house not made with hands, eternal in the heavens (2 Corinthians 5:1)."* **(See Mansion)**

Incense (Prayer): And he put the golden altar in the tent of the congregation before the vail: And he burnt sweet incense thereon; as the Lord commanded Moses (Exodus 40:26-27).

Ironing (Pressure from a trial): *"That he might present it to himself a glorious church, not having spot, or wrinkle, or any such thing; but that it should be holy and without blemish (Ephesians 5:27)."*

Island (Heaven): When men are cast down, then thou shalt say, *"There is lifting up; and he shall save the humble person. He shall deliver the island of the innocent: and it is delivered by the pureness of thine hands (Job 22:29-30)."*

Jewels (Gifts from God): *"I will greatly rejoice in the Lord, my soul shall be joyful in my God; for he hath clothed me with the garments of salvation, he hath covered me with the robe of righteousness, as a bridegroom decketh himself with ornaments, and as a bride adorneth herself with her jewels (Isaiah 61:10)."*

Key (Knowledge): *"And I will give unto thee the keys of the kingdom of heaven: and whatsoever thou shalt bind on earth shall be bound in heaven: and whatsoever thou shalt loose on earth shall be loosed in heaven (Mathew 16:19)."*

Kiss (Blood Covenant/Betrayal): *"And he came near, and kissed him: and he smelled the smell of his raiment, and blessed him, and said, See, the smell of my son is as the smell of a field which the Lord hath blessed (Genesis 27:27)."*

(Betrayal): *"Whomsoever I shall kiss, that same is he: hold him fast."* And forthwith he came to Jesus, and said, *"Hail, master;"* and kissed him. And Jesus said unto him, *"Friend, wherefore art thou come (Mathew 26:48-49)?"*

Kitchen (*Intents* of the heart; the kitchen is the heart of the home): *"For the word of God is quick, and powerful, and sharper than any twoedged sword, piercing even to the dividing asunder* *of soul and spirit, and of the joints and marrow, and is a discerner of the thoughts and intents of the heart (Hebrews 4:12)."*

Knees (Submission): *"For it is written, as I live,* saith the Lord, *every knee shall bow to me, and every tongue shall confess to God (Romans 14:11)."*

Knives (See Sword)

Ladder (Jesus is the one and only way to God): Jesus answered and said unto him, *"Because I said unto thee, I saw thee under the fig tree, believest thou? Thou shalt see greater things than these."* And he saith unto him, *"Verily, verily, I say unto you, Hereafter ye shall see heaven open, and the angels of God ascending and descending upon the Son of man (John 1:50-51)."*

And he dreamed, and behold a ladder set up on the earth, and the top of it reached to heaven: and behold the angels of God ascending and descending on it. And, behold, the Lord stood above it, and said, *"I am the Lord God of Abraham thy father, and the God of Isaac: the land whereon thou liest, to thee will I give it, and to thy seed (Genesis 28:12-13)."*

Lambs book of life (God's account of the righteous who will spend eternity in Heaven): And there shall in no wise enter into it anything that defileth, neither whatsoever worketh abomination, or maketh a lie: but they which are written in the Lamb's book of life (Revelation 21:27).

Lamp (Word of God): *"Thy word is a lamp unto my feet, and a light unto my path (Psalm 119:105)."*

Leaves, Green (Healing/Life): In the midst of the street of it, and on either side of the river, was there the tree of life, which bare twelve manner of fruits, and yielded her fruit every month: and the leaves of the tree were for the healing of the nations (Revelation 22:2).

Legs (To follow the Lord): *"The Lord is my shepherd; I shall not want. He maketh me to lie down in green pastures: he leadeth me beside the still waters. He restoreth my soul: he leadeth me in the paths of righteousness for his name's sake. Yea, though I walk through the valley of the shadow of death, I will fear no evil: for thou art with me; thy rod and thy staff they comfort me. Thou preparest a table before me in the presence of mine enemies: thou anointest my head with oil; my cup runneth over. Surely goodness and mercy shall follow me all the days of my life: and I will dwell in the house of the Lord for ever (Psalm 23)."*

Library (Knowledge): Study to shew thyself approved unto God, a workman that needeth not to be ashamed, rightly dividing the word of truth (2 Timothy 2:15).

Light (See Lamp)

Lightning (God's judgment): And the seventy returned again with joy, saying, *"Lord, even the devils are subject unto us through thy name."* And he said unto them, *"I beheld Satan as lightning fall from heaven (Luke 10:17-18)."*

Mansion (Jesus has prepared a mansion for you in Heaven): *"In my Father's house are many mansions: if it were not so, I would have told you. I go to prepare a place for you (John 14:2)."*

Map (God's laws are the path to Heaven): *"For the commandment is a lamp; and the law is light; and reproofs of instruction are the way of life (Proverbs 6:23)."*

Marriage (To the Jesus/Or Earthly Marriage): *"Let us be glad and rejoice, and give honour to him: for the marriage of the Lamb is come, and his wife hath made herself ready (Revelation 19:7)."*

For we are members of his body, of his flesh, and of his bones. For this cause shall a man leave his father and mother, and shall be joined unto his wife, and they two shall be one flesh. This is a great mystery: but I speak concerning

Christ and the church. Nevertheless let every one of you in particular so love his wife even as himself; and the wife see that she reverence her husband (Ephesians 5:30-33).

Maze (the "battle" that you face throughout your life): And Moses said unto them, *"If the children of Gad and the children of Reuben will pass with you over Jordan, every man armed to battle, before the Lord, and the land shall be subdued before you; then ye shall give them the land of Gilead for a possession (Numbers 32:29)."*

Measuring Cup (Level of Faith in God): *"If any man have ears to hear, let him hear."* And he said unto them, *"Take heed what ye hear: with what measure ye mete, it shall be measured to you: and unto you that hear shall more be given. For he that hath, to him shall be given: and he that hath not, from him shall be taken even that which he hath (Mathew 4:23-25)."*

Microphone (Voice of God): *"What I tell you in darkness, that speak ye in light: and what ye hear in the ear, that preach ye upon the housetops (Mathew 10:27)."*

Mirror (Reflection of your spirit, in Jesus Christ): *"For which cause we faint not; but though our outward man perish, yet the inward man is renewed day by day. For our light affliction, which is but for a moment, worketh for us a far more exceeding and eternal weight of glory; While we look not at the things which are seen, but at the things which are not seen: for the things which are seen are temporal; but the things which are not seen are eternal (2 Corinthians 4:16-18)."*

Money (The love of money is the root of all evil): *"For the love of money is the root of all evil: which while some coveted after, they have erred from the faith, and pierced themselves through with many sorrows (1 Timothy 6:10)."*

Moon (The Church): *"Moreover the light of the moon shall be as the light of the sun, and the light of the sun shall be sevenfold, as the* *light of seven days, in the day that the Lord bindeth up the breach of his people, and healeth the stroke of their wound (Isaiah 30:26)."*

Mountain (Obstacle to overcome): And Jesus said unto them, *"Because of your unbelief: for verily I say unto you, If ye have faith as a grain of mustard seed, ye shall say unto this mountain, Remove hence to yonder place; and it shall remove; and nothing shall be impossible unto you (Mathew 17:20)."*

Neck (Stiff-necked people): *"For I know thy rebellion, and thy stiff neck: behold, while I am yet alive with you this day, ye have been rebellious against the Lord; and how much more after my death (Deuteronomy 31:27)."*

Net (Used to separate the good and evil): *"Again, the kingdom of heaven is like unto a net, that was cast into the sea, and gathered of every kind: Which, when it was full, they drew to shore, and sat down, and gathered the good into vessels, but cast the bad away. So shall it be at the end of the world: the angels shall come forth, and sever the wicked from among the just, and shall cast them into the furnace of fire: there shall be wailing and gnashing of teeth (Mathew 13:47-50)."*

New Car (New ministry/or job): And he made him to ride in the second chariot which he had; and they cried before him, *"Bow the knee"*: and he made him ruler over all the land of Egypt (Genesis 41:40-43).

Newspaper (Announcement): *"For nothing is secret, that shall not be made manifest; neither anything hid, that shall not be known and come abroad (Luke 8:17)."*

Nose (Discern): *"They have ears, but they hear not: noses have they, but they smell not (Psalm 115:6)."*

Nudity (to walk in the flesh): *"Behold, I come as a thief. Blessed is he that watcheth, and keepeth his garments, lest he walk naked, and they see his shame (Revelation 16:15)."*

Oil, Holy (Holy unto the Lord): And the Lord said unto Moses, *"Take unto thee sweet spices, stacte, and onlycha, and galbanum; these sweet spices with pure frankincense: of each shall there be a like weight: And thou shalt make it a perfume, a confection after the art of the apothecary, tempered together, pure and holy: And thou shalt beat some of it very small, and put of it before the testimony in the tabernacle of the congregation, where I will meet with thee: it shall be unto you most holy. And as for the perfume which thou shalt make, ye shall not make to yourselves according to the composition thereof: it shall be unto thee holy for the Lord (Exodus 30:34-37)."*

Oven (Heart): *"For they have made ready their heart like an oven, whiles they lie in wait: their baker sleepeth all the night; in the morning it burneth as a flaming fire (Hosea 7:6)."*

Paint & Paint brush (Blood of Jesus covers all sin): *"Even the righteousness of God which is by faith of Jesus Christ unto all and upon all them that believe: for there is no difference: For all have sinned, and come short of the glory of God; Being justified freely by his grace through the redemption that is in Christ Jesus: Whom God hath set forth to be a propitiation through faith in his blood, to declare his righteousness for the remission of sins that are past, through the forbearance of God (Romans 3:22-25)."*

FYI: The Lord showed me a vision once after the call was made for repentance, in this vision I saw angels ministering; one angel had a paint bucket with blood and would dip the paint brush into the bucket then cover the person from head to toe in one big swoosh and all the angels were excited with joy for the repentance! Oh the blood of Jesus washes us white as snow, glory to God in the highest!

Park (Rest): *"But now the Lord my God hath given me rest on every side, so that there is neither adversary nor evil occurrent (1 Kings 5:4)."*

Pearl (Kingdom of Heaven): *"Again, the kingdom of heaven is like unto treasure hid in a field; the which when a man hath found, he hideth, and for joy thereof goeth and selleth all that he hath, and buyeth that field. Again, the kingdom of heaven is like unto a merchant man, seeking goodly pearls: Who, when he had found one pearl of great price, went and sold all that he had, and bought it (Mathew 13:44-46)."*

Perfume (See Oil, Holy)

Picture (Memory): *"Then ye shall drive out all the inhabitants of the land from before you, and destroy all their pictures, and destroy all their molten images, and quite pluck down all their high places (Numbers 33:52)."*

Pillars (Overcomer): *"Him that overcometh will I make a pillar in the temple of my God, and he shall go no more out: and I will write upon him the name of my God, and the name of the city of my God, which is new Jerusalem, which cometh down out of heaven from my God: and I will write upon him my new name (Revelation 3:12)."*

Pit (Hell): *"The wicked shall be turned into hell and all the nations that forget God (Psalm 9:17)."*

Plow/Plowman (The remnant): *"In that day will I raise up the tabernacle of David that is fallen, and close up the breaches thereof; and I will raise up his ruins, and I will build it as in the days of old: That they may possess the remnant of Edom, and of all the heathen, which are called by my name,"* saith the Lord that doeth this. *"Behold, the days come,* saith the Lord, *that the plowman shall overtake the reaper, and the treader of grapes him that soweth seed; and the mountains shall drop sweet wine, and all the hills shall melt. And I will bring again the captivity of my* *people of Israel, and they shall build the waste cities, and inhabit them; and they shall plant vineyards, and drink the wine thereof; they shall also make gardens, and eat the fruit of them. And I will plant them upon their land, and they shall no more be pulled up out of their land which I have given them,"* saith the Lord thy God (Amos 9:11-17).

Postage Stamp (Covenant): *"Labour not for the meat which perisheth, but for that meat which endureth unto everlasting life, which the Son of man shall give unto you: for him hath God the Father sealed (John 6:27)."*

Pot/Dish (God's Judgement): *"And I will stretch over Jerusalem the line of Samaria, and the plummet of the house of Ahab: and I will wipe Jerusalem as a man wipeth a dish, wiping it, and turning it upside down (2 Kings 21:13)."*

Pregnancy (New ministry, this dream can happen to a woman or a man/Be patient waiting for the gifts to be released from God): *"Having then gifts differing according to the grace that is given to us, whether prophecy, let us prophesy according to the proportion of faith; Or ministry, let us wait on our ministering: or he that teacheth, on teaching; Or he that exhorteth, on exhortation: he that giveth, let him do it with simplicity; he that ruleth, with diligence; he that sheweth mercy, with cheerfulness. Let love be without dissimulation. Abhor that which is evil; cleave to that which is good. Be kindly affectioned one to another with brotherly love; in honour preferring one another; Not slothful in business; fervent in spirit; serving the Lord (Romans 12:6-11)."*

Prison (Bondage to sin): *"And deliver them who through fear of death were all their lifetime subject to bondage (Hebrews 2:15)."*

Purse (Treasure): *"But lay up for yourselves treasures in heaven, where neither moth nor rust doth corrupt, and where thieves do not break through nor steal: For where your treasure is, there will your heart* be also. *The light of the body is the eye: if therefore thine eye be single, thy whole body shall be full of light (Mathew 6:20-22)."*

Radio (Sing to the Lord): *"My lips shall greatly rejoice when I sing unto thee; and my soul, which thou hast redeemed (Psalm 71:23)."*

Raft (Drifting/without direction): *"That we henceforth be no more children, tossed to and fro, and carried about with every wind of doctrine, by the sleight of men, and cunning craftiness, whereby they lie in wait to deceive (Ephesians 4:14)."*

Railroad Track ("Stay on track"): *"Because strait is the gate, and narrow is the way, which leadeth unto life, and few there be that find it (Matthew 7:14)."*

Rain (Life/Holy Spirit/Restoration): *"Ask ye of the Lord rain in the time of the latter rain; so the Lord shall make bright clouds, and give them showers of rain, to everyone grass in the field (Zechariah 10:1)."*

Rainbow (God's Covenant not to flood the earth again): *"I do set my bow in the cloud, and it shall be for a token of a covenant between me and the earth. And it shall come to pass, when I bring a cloud over the earth, that the bow shall be seen in the cloud: And I will remember my covenant, which is between me and you and every living creature of all flesh; and the waters shall no more become a flood to destroy all flesh (Genesis 9:13-15)."*

Rape (Violation): Howbeit he would not hearken unto her voice: but, being stronger than she, forced her, and lay with her (2 Samuel 13:14).

Rapture (Jesus Christ returns to receive his faithful children!): *"For if we believe that Jesus died and rose again, even so them also which sleep in Jesus will God bring with him. For this we say unto you by the word of the Lord, that we which are alive and remain unto the coming of the Lord shall not prevent them which are asleep. For the Lord himself shall descend from heaven* *with a shout, with the voice of the archangel, and with the trump of God: and the dead in Christ shall rise first: Then we which are alive and remain shall be caught up together with them in the clouds, to meet the Lord in the air: and so shall we ever be with the Lord. Wherefore comfort one another with these words (1 Thessalonians 4:14-18)."*

Rearview Mirror (Forget the past or you will not enter the Kingdom of God): And Jesus said unto him, *"No man, having put his hand to the plough, and looking back, is fit for the kingdom of God (Luke 9:62)."*

Refrigerator (Heart): A good man out of the good treasure of the heart bringeth forth good things: and an evil man out of the evil treasure bringeth forth evil things (Mathew 12:35).

FYI: God will use different vessels that he has placed upon this Earth to speak with us, food and drink is kept in the refrigerator, we eat and our heart is content physically, when we spiritually eat and drink God's (Heart) for us we are spiritually content as well.

Rings (The "wheels" of the four living creatures were also called "Rings"/to decree with a ring): *"When they went, they went upon their four sides: and they turned not when they went. As for their rings, they were so high that they were dreadful; and their rings were full of eyes round about them four. And when the living creatures went, the wheels went by them: and when the living creatures were lifted up from the earth, the wheels were lifted up (Ezekiel 1:17-19)."*

(To decree with a ring): *"Write ye also for the Jews, as it liketh you, in the king's name, and seal it with the king's ring: for the writing which is written in the king's name, and sealed with the king's ring, may no man reverse (Esther 8:8)."*

River (Refuge and strength): *"Though the waters thereof roar and be troubled, though the mountains shake with the swelling thereof. Selah. There is a river, the streams whereof shall make glad the city of God, the holy place of the tabernacles of the most High (Psalm 46:3-4)."*

Robe (Righteousness/Royalty): *"His eyes were as a flame of fire, and on his head were many crowns; and he had a name written, that no man knew, but he himself. And he was clothed with a vesture dipped in blood: and his name is called The Word of God. And the armies which were in heaven followed him upon white horses, clothed in fine linen, white and clean (Revelation 19:12-14)."*

Rock (See Fortress)

Rod (God's Judgement/God's provision): And Moses and Aaron did so, as the Lord commanded; and he lifted up the rod, and smote the waters that were in the river, in the sight of Pharaoh, and in the sight of his servants; and all the waters that were in the river were turned to blood. And the fish that was in the river died; and the river stank, and the Egyptians could not drink of the water of the river; and there was blood throughout all the land of Egypt (Exodus 7:19-21).

(God's provision): And the Lord said unto Moses, *"Wherefore criest thou unto me? speak unto the children of Israel, that they go forward: But lift thou up thy rod, and stretch out thine hand over the sea, and divide it: and the children of Israel shall go on dry ground through the midst of the sea. And I, behold, I will harden the hearts of the Egyptians, and they shall follow them: and I will get me honour upon Pharaoh, and upon all his host, upon his chariots, and upon his horsemen (Exodus 14:15-17)."*

Roller Coaster (Double-minded man will not receive anything of the Lord): *"But let him ask in faith, nothing wavering. For he that wavereth is like a wave of the sea driven with the wind and tossed.*

For let not that man think that he shall receive anything of the Lord. A double minded man is unstable in all his ways (James 1:6-8)."

Roller Skates (Swift advancement): *"For he will finish the work, and cut it short in righteousness: because a short work will the Lord make upon the earth (Romans 9:28)."*

Roof (The council of God to preach from the rooftops/Preach the gospel, tell everyone): *"What I tell you in darkness, that speak ye in light: and what ye hear in the ear, that preach ye upon the house-tops (Mathew 10:27)."*

Roots of a tree base, the (Your faith established in Jesus Christ): And ye have therefore received Christ Jesus the Lord, so walk ye in him: Rooted and built up in him, and stablished in the faith, as ye have been taught, abounding therein with thanks-giving (Colossians 2:6-7).

Rope (Sampson had the strength of God from physical bondage/Egypt was a house of bondage/Bondage to sin): And Delilah said unto Samson, *"Behold, thou hast mocked me, and told me lies: now tell me, I pray thee, wherewith thou mightest be bound."* And he said unto her, *"If they bind me fast with new ropes that never were occupied, then shall I be weak, and be as another man."* Delilah therefore took new ropes, and bound him therewith, and said unto him, *"The Philistines be upon thee, Samson. And there were liers in wait abiding in the chamber."* And he brake them from off his arms like a thread (Judges 16:10-13).

(Egypt was a house of bondage): And the people answered and said, *"God forbid that we should forsake the Lord, to serve other gods; For the Lord our God, he it is that brought us up and our fathers out of the land of Egypt, from the house of bondage, and which did those great signs in our sight, and preserved us in all the way wherein we went, and among all the people through whom we passed: And the Lord drave out from before us all the people, even the Amorites which dwelt in the land: therefore will we also serve the Lord; for he is our God (Joshua 24:16-18)."*

(Bondage to sin): *"For I acknowledge my transgressions: and my sin is ever before me. Against thee, thee only, have I sinned, and done this evil in thy sight: that thou mightest be justified when thou speakest, and be clear when thou judgest. Behold, I was shapen in iniquity; and in sin did my mother conceive me. Behold, thou desirest truth in the inward parts: and in the hidden part thou shalt make me to know wisdom. Purge me with hyssop, and I shall be clean: wash me, and I shall be whiter than snow. Make me to hear joy and gladness; that the bones which thou hast broken may rejoice (Psalm 51:3-8)."*

Rug: (To sweep under the *rug*/God sees all sin): *"For there is nothing hid, which shall not be manifested; neither was anything kept secret, but that it should come abroad (Mark 4:22)."*

Running (Strive to receive the Kingdom of God): *"Know ye not that they which run in a race run all, but one receiveth the prize? So run, that ye may obtain (1 Corinthians 9:24)."*

Sand (God will multiply thy seed like the sand, a covenant promise God made with Abraham; this is a generational blessing from God): And said, *"By myself have I sworn, saith the Lord, for because thou hast done this thing, and hast not withheld thy son, thine only son: That in blessing I will bless thee, and in multiplying I will multiply thy seed as the stars of the heaven, and as the sand which is upon the sea shore; and thy seed shall possess the gate of his enemies; And in thy seed shall all the nations of the earth be blessed; because thou hast obeyed my voice (Genesis 22:16-18)."*

School (Teaching ministry in a church or school): And he went into the synagogue, and spake boldly for the space of three months, disputing and persuading the things concerning the kingdom of God (Acts 19:8).

Sea (Humanity/Spirit of the World): *"And I saw a new heaven and a new earth: for the first heaven and the first earth were passed away; and there was no more sea. And I John saw the holy city, new Jerusalem, coming down from God out of heaven, prepared as a bride adorned for her husband. And I heard a great voice out of heaven saying, Behold, the tabernacle of God is with men, and he will dwell with them, and they shall be his people, and God himself shall be with them, and be their God (Revelation 21:1-3)."*

Sea Coast (The boundary line where the "unrighteous" who are captive in the sea (Hell), can't enter eternity in Heaven): *"Hear now this, O foolish people, and without understanding; which have eyes, and see not; which have ears, and hear not: Fear ye not me?* Saith the Lord: *will ye not tremble at my presence, which have placed the sand for the bound of the sea by the perpetual decree, that it cannot pass it: and though the waves thereof toss themselves, yet can they not prevail; though they roar, yet can they not pass over it (Jeremiah 5:21-22)?"*

Sea of glass (God will make your enemy your footstool): The Lord said unto my Lord, *"Sit thou at my right hand, until I make thine enemies thy footstool (Psalm 110:1)."*

"And before the throne there was a sea of glass like unto crystal: and in the midst of the throne, and round about the throne, were four beasts full of eyes before and behind (Revelation 4:6)."

Seed (Word of God): Now the parable is this: *"The seed is the word of God. Those by the way side are they that hear; then cometh the devil, and taketh away the word out of their hearts, lest they should believe and be saved. They on the rock are they, which, when they hear, receive the word with joy; and these have no root, which for a while believe, and in time of temptation fall away. And that which fell among thorns are they, which, when they have heard, go forth, and are choked with cares and riches and pleasures of this life, and bring no fruit to perfection. But* *that on the good ground are they, which in an honest and good heart, having heard the word, keep it, and bring forth fruit with patience (Luke 8:11-15)."*

Sewage (Corruption): *"For he that soweth to his flesh shall of the flesh reap corruption; but he that soweth to the Spirit shall of the Spirit reap life everlasting (Galatians 6:8)."*

Sewing (Reconciliation): And it came to pass, when he had made an end of speaking unto Saul, that the soul of Jonathan was knit with the soul of David, and Jonathan loved him as his own soul (1 Samuel 18:1).

Sex (Agreement/Covenant/Unity): I say therefore to the unmarried and widows, it is good for them if they abide even as I. But if they cannot contain, let them marry: for it is better to marry than to burn (1 Corinthians 7:8-9).

For we are members of his body, of his flesh, and of his bones. For this cause shall a man leave his father and mother, and shall be joined unto his wife, and they two shall be one flesh. This is a great mystery: but I speak concerning Christ and the church. Nevertheless let every one of you in particular so love his wife even as himself; and the wife see that she reverence her husband (Ephesians 5:30-33).

Shield of Faith (The shield of faith protects you from any doubt that Satan tries to send your way): Above all, taking the shield of faith, wherewith ye shall be able to quench all the fiery darts of the wicked (Ephesians 6:16).

Shelf or Shelves (To place God on a shelf to use later taking his name in vain; the third of the Ten Commandments): *"Thou shalt not take the name of the Lord thy God in vain; for the Lord will not hold him guiltless that taketh his name in vain (Exodus 20:7)."*

Ship (See Boat/Ship/Shipwreck)

Shoes/Boots (Words/Spiritual Warfare): And your feet shod with the preparation of the gospel of peace (Ephesians 6:15).

This I say then, Walk in the Spirit, and ye shall not fulfil the lust of the flesh (Galatians 5:16).

Shoulder (s) (Bearing your burdens or someone else's): Casting all your care upon him; for he careth for you. Be sober, be vigilant; because your adversary the devil, as a roaring lion, walketh about, seeking whom he may devour: Whom resist stedfast in the faith, knowing that the same afflictions are accomplished in your brethren that are in the world. But the God of all grace, who hath called us unto his eternal glory by Christ Jesus, after that ye have suffered a while, make you perfect, stablish, strengthen, settle you. To him be glory and dominion forever and ever. Amen (1 Peter 5:7-11).

Skiing, Water (To have faith or not to have faith): And he said, *"Come."* And when Peter was come down out of the ship, he walked on the water, to go to Jesus. But when he saw the wind boisterous, he was afraid; and beginning to sink, he cried, saying, *"Lord, save me."* And immediately Jesus stretched forth his hand, and caught him, and said unto him, *"O thou of little faith, wherefore didst thou doubt (Mathew 14:29-31)?"*

Shovel (Dig deep of your sin and repent): And thou shalt have a paddle upon thy weapon; and it shall be, when thou wilt ease thyself abroad, thou shalt dig therewith, and shalt turn back and cover that which cometh from thee (Deuteronomy 23:13).

Sleep (Unconscious/hidden/death): For the Lord hath poured out upon you the spirit of deep sleep, and hath closed your eyes: the prophets and your rulers, the seers hath he covered (Isaiah 29:10).

And that, knowing the time, that now it is high time to awake out of sleep: for now is our salvation nearer than when we believed (Romans 13:11).

Square (Legalistic/Religious/religion/hard/of the world): And when ye reap the harvest of your land, thou shalt not wholly reap the corners of thy field, neither shalt thou gather the gleanings of thy harvest (Leviticus 19:9).

Smoke (Manifest Presence): And one cried unto another, and said, *"Holy, holy, holy, is the Lord of hosts: the whole earth is full of his glory."* And the posts of the door moved at the voice of him that cried, and the house was filled with smoke (Isaiah 6:3-4).

Socks (To put on or take off the covering of God): And your feet shod with the preparation of the gospel of peace (Ephesians 6:15).

Steal, to (Thou shalt not steal is the eighth of the Ten Commandments): Thou shalt not steal (Exodus 20:15).

Steps (Walking in righteousness): Yea, the Lord shall give that which is good; and our land shall yield her increase. Righteousness shall go before him; and shall set us in the way of his steps (Psalm 85:12-13).

Sweeping (Repentance/removing obstacles): Having therefore these promises, dearly beloved, let us cleanse ourselves from all filthiness of the flesh and spirit, perfecting holiness in the fear of God (2 Corinthians 7:1).

"For behold this selfsame thing, that ye sorrowed after a godly sort, what carefulness it wrought in you, yea, what clearing of yourselves, yea, what indignation, yea, what fear, yea, what vehement desire, yea, what zeal, yea, what revenge! In all things ye have approved yourselves to be clear in this matter (2 Corinthians 7:11)."

Jesus answered and said unto them, Verily I say unto you, *"If ye have faith, and doubt not, ye shall not only do this which is done to the fig tree, but also if ye shall say unto this mountain, Be thou removed, and be thou cast into the sea; it shall be done (Mathew 21:21)."*

Swimming (God's Holy Spirit being poured out without measure for the righteous) Afterward he measured a thousand; and it was a river that I could not pass over: for the waters were risen, waters to swim in, a river that could not be passed over (Ezekiel 47:5).

Sword (The word of God/False prophets shall die by the sword): And take the helmet of salvation, and the sword of the Spirit, which is the word of God (Ephesians 6:17).

But if ye refuse and rebel, ye shall be devoured with the sword: for the mouth of the Lord hath spoken it (Isaiah 1:20).

Then said I, Ah, Lord God! behold, the prophets say unto them, Ye shall not see the sword, neither shall ye have famine; but I will give you assured peace in this place. Then the Lord said unto me, The prophets prophesy lies in my name: I sent them not, neither have I commanded them, neither spake unto them: they prophesy unto you a false vision and divination, and a thing of nought, and the deceit of their heart. Therefore thus saith the Lord concerning the prophets that prophesy in my name, and I sent them not, yet they say, Sword and famine shall not be in this land; By sword and famine shall those prophets be consumed (Jeremiah 14:13-15).

Telephone, to receive a call or to call on the (God talking to you or you talking to God to receive or send a message for yourself or for another person, depends on the content of the dream): And Moses said, I will now turn aside, and see this great sight, why the bush is not burnt. And when the Lord saw that he turned aside to see, God called unto him out of the midst of the bush, and said, Moses, Moses. And he said, Here am I. And he said, Draw not nigh hither: put off thy shoes from off thy feet, for the place whereon thou standest is holy ground (Exodus 3:3-5).

In my distress I called upon the Lord, and cried to my God: and he did hear my voice out of his temple, and my cry did enter into his ears. Then the earth shook and trembled; the foundations of heaven moved and shook, because he was wroth. There went up a smoke out of his nostrils, and fire out of his mouth devoured: coals were kindled by it. He bowed the heavens also, and came down; and darkness was under his feet. And he rode upon a cherub, and did fly: and he was seen upon the wings of the wind 2 Samuel 22:7-11).

Television (Vision/Message/prophecy/preaching/news): Then thou scarest me with dreams, and terrifiest me through visions (Job 7:14).

Then was the secret revealed unto Daniel in a night vision. Then Daniel blessed the God of heaven (Daniel 2:19).

Thorns (Sin/See the Crown of Thorns): They shall call the nobles thereof to the kingdom, but none shall be there, and all her princes shall be nothing. And thorns shall come up in her palaces, nettles and brambles in the fortresses thereof: and it shall be an habitation of dragons, and a court for owls. The wild beasts of the desert shall also meet with the wild beasts of the island, and the satyr shall cry to his fellow; the screech owl also shall rest there, and find for herself a place of rest (Isaiah 34:12-14).

Title/Deed (Ownership/possession): And the field, and the cave that is therein, were made sure unto Abraham for a possession of a buryingplace by the sons of Heth (Genesis 23:20).

Tongues (The fire of the Holy Spirit): And they were all filled with the Holy Ghost, and began to speak with other tongues, as the Spirit gave them utterance (Acts 2:4:1).

(A gift from God/Interpretation of tongues): To another the working of miracles; to another prophecy; to another discerning of spirits; to another divers kinds of tongues; to another the interpretation of tongues: But all these worketh that one and the self-same Spirit, dividing to every man severally as he will (Corinthians 12:10-11).

(Interpretation of tongues for the edification of the body of Christ): He that speaketh in an unknown tongue edifieth himself; but he that prophesieth edifieth the church. I would that ye all spake with tongues, but prophesieth than he that speaketh with tongues, except he interpret, that the church may receive edifying (Corinthians 14:5).

(The tongue is full of deadly poison and can cause the whole body to be in sin): And the tongue is a fire, a world of iniquity: so is the tongue among our members, that it defileth the whole body, and setteth on fire the course of nature; and it is set on fire of hell. For every kind of beasts, and of birds, and of serpents, and of things in the sea, is tamed, and hath been tamed of mankind: But the tongue can no man tame; it is an unruly evil, full of deadly poison (James 3:6-8).

Tooth (Broken tooth means to be without confidence): Confidence in an unfaithful man in time of trouble is like a broken tooth, and a foot out of joint (Proverbs 25:19).

Tornados (Judgement of God for the unrighteous and the righteous): (the unrighteous): God is jealous, and the Lord revengeth; the Lord revengeth, and is furious; the Lord will take vengeance on his adversaries, and he reserveth wrath for his enemies. The Lord is slow to anger, and great in power, and will not at all acquit the wicked: the Lord hath his way in the whirlwind and in the storm, and the clouds are the dust of his feet. He rebuketh the sea, and maketh it dry, and drieth up all the rivers: Bashan languisheth, and Carmel, and the flower of Lebanon languisheth (Nahum 1:2-4).

(the righteous): Now it came to pass on a certain day, that he went into a ship with his disciples: and he said unto them, Let us go over unto the other side of the lake. And they launched forth. But as they sailed he fell asleep: and there came down a storm of wind on the lake; and they were filled with water, and were in jeopardy. And they came to him, and awoke him, saying, Master, master, we perish. Then he arose, and rebuked the wind and the raging of the water: and they ceased, and there was a calm (Luke 8:22:24).

Tractor (To plow in hope): Or saith he it altogether for our sakes? For our sakes, no doubt, this is written: that he that ploweth should plow in hope; and he that thresheth in hope should partake of his hope (1 Corinthians 9:10).

Tree (Saints who are walking with God): Blessed is the man that walketh not in the counsel of the undgodly, nor standeth in the way of sinners, nor sitteth in the seat of the scornful. But his delight is in the law of the Lord; and his law doth he meditate day and night. And he shall be like a tree planted by the rivers of the water, that bringeth forth his fruit in his season; his leaf also shall not wither; and whatsoever he doeth shall prosper (Psalm 1:1-3).

Tree Stump (roots/tenacious/hope/new beginning): For there is hope of a tree, if it be cut down, that it will sprout again, and that the tender branch thereof will not cease. Though the root thereof wax old in the earth, and the stock thereof die in the ground; Yet through the scent of water it will bud, and bring forth boughs like a plant (Job 14:7-9).

Tunnel/Conduit ("King Hezekiah" had a tunnel built so that the people of Jerusalem would have water when the Assyrians attacked them): And the rest of the acts of Hezekiah, and all his might, and how he made a pool, and a conduit, and brought water into the city, are they not written in the book of the chronicles of the kings of Judah (2 Kings 20:20).

Urinate/the natural need to (Argument/Strife): The beginning of strife is as when one letteth out water: therefore leave off contention, before it be meddled with (Proverbs 17:14).

USA (To see the Outline of the United States of America with every state within marked with the fire of the Father, and the Son, and of the Holy Ghost): And Jesus came and spake unto them, saying, *"All power is given unto me in heaven and in earth. Go ye therefore, and teach all nations, baptizing them in the name of the Father, and of the Son, and of the Holy Ghost: Teaching them to observe all things whatsoever I have commanded you: and, lo, I am with you always, even unto the end of the world. Amen (Mathew 28:18-20)."*

Vessels (Saints): Nevertheless the foundation of God standeth sure, having this seal, the Lord knoweth them that are his. And, let every one that nameth the name of Christ depart from iniquity. But in a great house there are not only vessels of gold and of silver, but also of wood and of earth; and some to honour, and some to dishonor. If a man therefore purge himself from these, he shall be a vessel unto honour, sanctified unto every good work (2 Timothy 2:19-21).

Walls, broken down or no (Not following Gods laws following your own spirit): He that hath no rule over his own spirit is like a city that is broken down, and without walls (Proverbs 25:28).

Washcloth/To wash/shower/bathe (To cleanse): Purge me with hyssop, and I shall be clean: wash me, and I shall be whiter than snow (Psalm 51:7).

Watch (It's time to do what the Lord is saying for you to do, can be ministry or a dream that he is showing you/the season that you are in with the Lord): To everything there is a season, and a time to every purpose under the heaven: A time to be born, and a time to die; a time to plant, and a time to pluck up that which is planted; A time to kill, and a time to heal; a time to break down, and a time to build up; A time to weep, and a time to laugh; a time to mourn, and a time to dance; A time to cast away stones, and a time to gather stones together; a time to embrace, and a time to refrain from embracing; A time to get, and a time to lose; a time to keep, and a time to cast away; A time to rend, and a time to sew; a time to keep silence, and a time to speak; A time to love, and a time to hate; a time of war, and a time of peace. What profit hath he that worketh in that wherein he laboureth? I have seen the travail, which God hath given to the sons of men to be exercised in it. He hath made every thing beautiful in his time: also he hath set the world in their heart, so that no man can find out the work that God maketh from the beginning to the end (Ecclesiastes 3:1-11).

Water Baptism ("Water Baptism" is to be "Born Again" to be cleansed for the remission of sins once you receive the water baptism you receive the Holy Spirit): *"Verily, verily, I say unto thee, Except a man be born of water and of the Spirit, he cannot enter into the kingdom of God. That which is born of the flesh is flesh; and that which is born of the Spirit is spirit. Marvel not that I said unto thee, Ye must be born again. The wind bloweth where it listeth, and thou hearest the sound thereof, but canst not tell whence it cometh, and whither it goeth: so is every one that is born of the Spirit (John 3:5-8)."*

Water fountain or Well (God is Life Eternal): And he said unto me, *"It is done. I am Alpha and Omega, the beginning and the end. I will give unto him that is athirst of the fountain of the water of life freely (Revelation 21:6)."*

Western Town ("The wild west"/spiritual warfare): When thou comest nigh unto a city to fight against it, then proclaim peace unto it (Deuteronomy 20:10).

Wind (Holy Spirit): Jesus answered and said unto him, *"Verily, verily, I say unto thee, Except a man be born again, he cannot see the kingdom of God."* Nicodemus saith unto him, *"How can a man be born when he is old? can he enter the second time into his mother's womb, and be born?"* Jesus answered, *"Verily, verily, I say unto thee, Except a man be born of water and of the Spirit, he cannot enter into the kingdom of God. That which is born of the flesh is flesh; and that which is born of the Spirit is spirit. Marvel not that I said unto thee, Ye must be born again. The wind bloweth where it listeth, and thou hearest the sound thereof, but canst not tell whence it cometh, and whither it goeth: so is every one that is born of the Spirit (John 3:8-8)."*

Wine (Sin/Idol/habit and "Blood of Jesus" covers all sin): And be not drunk with wine, wherein is excess; but be filled with the Spirit (Ephesians 5:18).

For the time past of our life may suffice us to have wrought the will of the Gentiles, when we walked in lasciviousness, lusts, excess of wine, revellings, banquetings, and abominable idolatries (1 Peter 4:3).

(Blood of Jesus covers all sin): And he took the cup, and gave thanks, and gave it to them, saying, Drink ye all of it; For this is my blood of the new testament, which is shed for many for the remission of sins. But I say unto you, I will not drink henceforth of this fruit of the vine, until that day when I drink it new with you in my Father's kingdom (Mathew 26:28).

Windows (God will pour out blessings upon you when you are faithful in tithing to your church): Bring ye all the tithes into the storehouse, that there may be meat in mine house, and prove me now herewith, saith the Lord of hosts, if I will not open you the windows of heaven, and pour you out a blessing, that there shall not be room enough to receive it (Malachi 3:10).

ENDNOTES

1   John 3:5-8 KJV

2   Luke 23:42-43 KJV

3   Mathew 7:21-23 KJV

4   Mathew 7:13-14 KJV

5   James 1:17 KJV

6   2 Corinthians 5:17 KJV

7   Mathew 5:13 KJV

8   1 Corinthians 6:17 KJV

9   1 Peter 2:9 KJV

10   Revelation 19:7 KJV

11   Revelation 3:19 KJV

12   Revelation 3:20-22 KJV

13   Ezekiel 11:5 KJV

14   1 Samuel 16:7 KJV

15   Mathew 7:15 KJV

16   Mark 4:22 KJV

17   James 2:23 KJV

18   2 Corinthians 2:14 KJV

19   Hebrews 11:6 KJV

20   The Merriam-Webster Dictionary, Merriam-Webster Incorporated, John M. Morse, President and Publisher 2004, page 219.

21   Daniel 2:31-35 KJV

22   Genesis 28:10-15 KJV

23   The Merriam-Webster Dictionary, Merriam-Webster Incorporated, John M. Morse, President and Publisher 2004, page 809.

24   Luke 24:36-43 KJV

25   Mathew 17:1-13 KJV

26   The Merriam-Webster Dictionary, Merriam-Webster Incorporated, John M. Morse, President and Publisher 2004, page 451.

27   The Merriam-Webster Dictionary, Merriam-Webster Incorporated, John M. Morse, President and Publisher 2004, page 522.

28   Mark 4:1-34 KJV

29   Mark 4:11-12 KJV

30   Mathew 13:13-15 KJV

31   John 10:27 KJV

32   1 Peter 3:22 KJV

33   Mark 6:3 KJV

34   Numbers 17:8-10 KJV

35   Exodus 4:20 KJV

36   Exodus 17:9 KJV

37   The Merriam-Webster Thesaurus, Merriam-Webster Incorporated, John M. Morse, President and Publisher 2005, page 661.

38   1 Peter 2:9 KJV

39   Psalm 119:148 KJV

40   Isaiah 43:19 KJV

41   Revelation 1:12-16 KJV

42   Revelation 19:6 KJV

43   Numbers 15:37-41 KJV

44   Isaiah 40:31 KJV

45   Romans 12:2 KJV

46   John 4:23-24 KJV

47   Job 22:28 KJV

48   The Prophet's Dictionary, The Ultimate Guide to Supernatural Wisdom by Paula A. Price, PH.D., Copyright 1999, 2002, 2006 by Paula A. Price. Whitaker House Publishers, page 71.

49   Bohemian Grove, Cult of Conspiracy by Mike Hanson, copyright 2004 by Mike Hanson. iUniverse, Inc. Publishers, pages 56-57.

50   Romans 1:22-23 KJV

51   James 1:5 KJV

52   The Merriam-Webster Dictionary, Merriam-Webster Incorporated, John M. Morse, President and Publisher 2004, page 33.

53   The Merriam-Webster Thesaurus, Merriam-Webster Incorporated, John M. Morse, President and Publisher 2005, page 554.

54   The Merriam-Webster Dictionary, Merriam-Webster Incorporated, John M. Morse, President and Publisher 2004, page 247.

55   The Merriam-Webster Dictionary, Merriam-Webster Incorporated, John M. Morse, President and Publisher 2004, page 247.

56   The Merriam-Webster Dictionary, Merriam-Webster Incorporated, John M. Morse, President and Publisher 2004, page 312.

57   Merriam-Webster Dictionary, Merriam-Webster Incorporated, John M. Morse, President and Publisher 2004, page 370.

58   2 Peter 1:16-21 KJV

59   The Merriam-Webster Dictionary, Merriam-Webster Incorporated, John M. Morse, President and Publisher 2004, page 527.

60   The Merriam-Webster Thesaurus, Merriam-Webster Incorporated, John M. Morse, President and Publisher 2005, page 694.

61   The Merriam-Webster Thesaurus, Merriam-Webster Incorporated, John M. Morse, President and Publisher 2005, page 540.

62   Ephesians 4:11-15 KJV

63   John 4:35 KJV

64   Luke 16:15-18 KJV

65   John 5:22-24 KJV

66   Luke 9:26-27 KJV

67   Luke 15:3-10 KJV

68   Hebrews 11:1 KJV

69   Hebrews 11:6 KJV

70   John 4:36-37 KJV

71   John 4:38 KJV

72   The Merriam-Webster Dictionary, Merriam-Webster Incorporated, John M. Morse, President and Publisher 2004, page 498.

73   John 4:36 KJV

74   John 5:19-20 KJV

75   Numbers 15:37-41 KJV

76   Mark 16:9-20 KJV

77   Mathew 5:45 KJV

78   John 8:12 KJV

79   Isaiah 60:1 KJV

80   1 Kings 17:2-6 KJV

81   2 Timothy 2:15 KJV

82   John 4:34 KJV

83   Proverbs 31:22 KJV

84   Revelation 19:8 KJV

85   Isaiah 61:10 KJV

86   Mathew 21:21-22 KJV

87   Psalm 37:3-7 KJV

88   John 19:5 KJV

89   Proverbs 31:22 KJV

90   Mathew 21:22 KJV

91   The Merriam-Webster Thesaurus, Merriam-Webster Incorporated, John M. Morse, President and Publisher 2005, page 391.

92   Mathew 7:7-8 KJV

93   1 John 5:13-15 KJV

94   The Merriam-Webster Dictionary, Merriam-Webster Incorporated, John M. Morse, President and Publisher 2004, page 3.

95   2 Corinthians 5:20 KJV

96   The Merriam-Webster Thesaurus, Merriam-Webster Incorporated, John M. Morse, President and Publisher 2005, page 25.

97   The Merriam-Webster Dictionary, Merriam-Webster Incorporated, John M. Morse, President and Publisher 2004, page 254.

98   The Merriam-Webster Dictionary, Merriam-Webster Incorporated, John M. Morse, President and Publisher 2004, page 552.

99   Luke 11:2-4 KJV

100 John 3:5-8 KJV

101 Psalm 89:20 KJV

102 Luke 11:11-13 KJV

103 Isaiah 7:15 KJV

104 1 Peter 2:2 KJV

105 Mathew 13:30 KJV

106 John 4:34

107 Mark 9:47-50 KJV

108 Galatians 5:22-26 KJV

109 Galatians 3:16 KJV

110 Mathew 13:33-36 KJV

111 Isaiah 40:31 KJV

112 Acts 2:3-4 KJV

113   Hebrews 4:12 KJV

114   John 3:5-8 KJV

115   Mark 1:13 KJV

116   Luke 22:43-44 KJV

117   Exodus 3:5 KJV

118   Zechariah 5:9 KJV

119   Revelation 12:7-9 KJV

120   100,000 + Baby Names by Bruce Lansky, copyright 2006, 2007, 2008, 2009 by Bruce Lansky. Published by Meadowbrook Press. Page 555.

121   Psalm 104:4 KJV

122   Revelation 12:3-4 KJV

123   Exodus 32:7-9 KJV

124   100,000 + Baby Names by Bruce Lansky, copyright 2006, 2007, 2008, 2009 by Bruce Lansky. Published by Meadowbrook Press. Page 509.

125   James 1:17 KJV

126   Psalm 91:11 KJV

127   Psalm 91:11 KJV

128   1 John 4:18 KJV

129   Proverbs 22:6 KJV

130   Psalm 25:9-15 KJV

131   John 3:16 KJV

132   John 3:5-7 KJV

133   Romans 3:10 KJV

134   Titus 3.5-7 KJV

135 Mathew 25:46 KJV

136 Mathew 16:26 KJV

137 Revelation 20:14-15 KJV

138 Mathew 13:47-50 KJV

139 Revelation 6:4 KJV

140 Isaiah 13:20:22 KJV

141 The Merriam-Webster Dictionary, Merriam-Webster Incorporated, John M. Morse, President and Publisher 2004, page 642.

142 Proverbs 7:9-19 KJV

143 Ephesians 6:15 KJV

144 Mathew 25:41 KJV

145 Mark 14:62 KJV

146 1 Peter 5:8 KJV

147 Isaiah 1:16 KJV

148 Mathew 18:28 KJV

149 Mathew 5:8 KJV

150 Mathew 13:42 KJV

151 Isaiah 51:20 KJV

152 Ezekiel 12:2 KJV

153 Hosea 7:8-9 KJV

154 John 15:6 KJV

155 1 John 4:18 KJV

156 Exodus 13:21 KJV

157 Psalm 91:9-11 KJV

158 Deuteronomy 5:15 KJV

159 Revelation 21:18-21 KJV

160 Jeremiah 1:5 KJV

161 Revelation 19:11-13 KJV

162 John 19:2-3 KJV

163 Daniel 12:4 KJV

164 James 1:5 KJV

165 Revelation 21:21 KJV

166 Galatians 5:22 KJV

167 Genesis 1:27 KJV

168 John 14:6-7 KJV

169 John 21:14-17 KJV

170 Mathew 13:13-23 KJV

BIBLIOGRAPHY

The Holy Bible King James Version
Copyright 1977, 1984, 2001 by Thomas Nelson, Inc.

The Merriam-Webster Dictionary
Merriam-Webster Incorporated, John M. Morse, President and
    Publisher 2004

The Merriam-Webster Thesaurus
Merriam-Webster Incorporated, John M. Morse, President and
    Publisher 2005

The Prophet's Dictionary, The Ultimate Guide to Supernatural
    Wisdom by Paula A. Price, PH.D. Copyright 1999, 2002,
    2006 by Paula A. Price. Whitaker House Publishers

Bohemian Grove, Cult of Conspiracy by Mike Hanson, copyright
    2004 by Mike Hanson. iUniverse, Inc. Publishers.

100,000 + Baby Names by Bruce Lansky, copyright 2006, 2007,
    2008, 2009 by Bruce Lansky. Published by Meadowbrook
    Press

AUTHOR BIOGRAPHY

I am a Psalmist who ministers the word of God through the prophetic song of the Lord, as well as an Evangelist for God speaking his word upon this dry and thirsty world, "Prepare the way of the Lord." I am called to sing and speak to the nations to bring those who are lost back inside the Gates of Heaven. I love teaching classes on the discernment of dreams and visions helping people to understand how God speaks with them, and therefore they are able to walk in the calling that God has placed upon their life. An Ordained Minister of M.A.P. International, and Founder of "The Grand Room International."

e|LIVE

listen|imagine|view|experience

AUDIO BOOK DOWNLOAD INCLUDED WITH THIS BOOK!

In your hands you hold a complete digital entertainment package. In addition to the paper version, you receive a free download of the audio version of this book. Simply use the code listed below when visiting our website. Once downloaded to your computer, you can listen to the book through your computer's speakers, burn it to an audio CD or save the file to your portable music device (such as Apple's popular iPod) and listen on the go!

How to get your free audio book digital download:

1. Visit www.tatepublishing.com and click on the e|LIVE logo on the home page.
2. Enter the following coupon code:
   c343-db29-7508-f129-a394-778e-5ef6-fef9
3. Download the audio book from your e|LIVE digital locker and begin enjoying your new digital entertainment package today!